ONE OF THE YEAR'S BEST BOOKS

**THE NEW YORKER • THE GUARDIAN • SUNDAY TIMES
DAILY MAIL • GOOD MORNING AMERICA • SHE READS**

PRAISE FOR *INSIDE OUT*

"Thoughtful, questioning . . .
sometimes shocking, but never salacious."
—*WALL STREET JOURNAL*

"Her story is equal parts adversity and resilience,
told with candor."
—*USA TODAY*

"Moore narrates, with the precision of a butcher's knife,
her divorces, addiction, and eventual isolation,
but from this she pulls forth her most potent character yet:
a fully formed, gives-no-fucks woman of wisdom."
—*LENA DUNHAM, HARPER'S BAZAAR*

"Entirely unexpected. . . . One of the most
relatable depictions of motherhood I've read."
—*NEW YORK MAGAZINE'S "THE CUT"*

"The actress gets candid in a way
few modern A-listers have. . . . Poignant."
—*PEOPLE*

"Fucking fantastic. . . . A testament to survival."
—HOWARD STERN

"You want juicy details? That's what you expect in a celebrity
memoir, and you certainly get them here. . . . But you also get
something you almost never find in a celebrity memoir: candor."
—*NEW YORK TIMES BOOK REVIEW*

#1 NEW YORK TIMES BESTSELLER

INSIDE OUT

INSIDE
OUT

A MEMOIR

DEMI
MOORE

HARPER ● PERENNIAL

NEW YORK ● LONDON ● TORONTO ● SYDNEY ● NEW DELHI ● AUCKLAND

HARPER ● PERENNIAL

A hardcover edition of this book was published by HarperCollins Publishers in 2019.

This is a work of nonfiction. The events and experiences detailed herein are all true and have been faithfully rendered as the author has remembered them, to the best of her ability. Some names, identities, and circumstances have been changed in order to protect the privacy and/or anonymity of the various individuals involved. Others have vetted the manuscript and confirmed its rendering of events.

HarperCollins books may be purchased for educational, business, or sales promotional use. For information, please email the Special Markets Department at SPsales@harpercollins.com.

Grateful acknowledgment is made for permission to reprint from the following:
"The Guest House" from *The Essential Rumi* by Coleman Barks. Copyright © 1995 by Coleman Barks. Reprinted by permission of Coleman Barks.
Excerpt in chapter 13 from *Vanity Fair*'s website reprinted courtesy of George Lois/VF © Condé Nast.

All photographs are courtesy of the author unless otherwise noted.

FIRST HARPER PERENNIAL EDITION PUBLISHED 2020.

Designed by Bonni Leon-Berman

Library of Congress Cataloging-in-Publication Data has been applied for.

ISBN 978-0-06-204954-4 (pbk.)

20 21 22 23 24   LSC   10 9 8 7 6 5 4 3 2 1

For my mother, my daughters, and my daughters' daughters

THE GUEST HOUSE

This being human is a guest house.
Every morning a new arrival.

A joy, a depression, a meanness,
some momentary awareness comes
as an unexpected visitor.

Welcome and entertain them all!
Even if they are a crowd of sorrows,
who violently sweep your house
empty of its furniture,
still, treat each guest honorably.
He may be clearing you out
for some new delight.

The dark thought, the shame, the malice.
meet them at the door laughing and invite them in.

Be grateful for whatever comes.
because each has been sent
as a guide from beyond.

—*Rumi (translated by Coleman Barks)*

CONTENTS

PROLOGUE

The same question kept going through my head: *How did I get here?*

In the empty house where I'd been married, where we'd added on because I had more kids than bedrooms, I was now completely alone. I was almost fifty. The husband who I'd thought was the love of my life had cheated on me and then decided he didn't want to work on our marriage. My children weren't speaking to me: no happy birthday calls, no Merry Christmas texts. Nothing. Their father—a friend I'd counted on for years—was gone from my life. The career I'd scrambled to create since I moved out of my mother's apartment when I was sixteen years old was stalled, or maybe it was over for good. Everything I was attached to—even my health—had abandoned me. I was getting blinding headaches and losing weight scarily fast. I looked like I felt: destroyed.

Is this life? I wondered. *Because if this is it, I'm done. I don't know what I'm doing here.*

I was going through the motions, doing whatever seemed like

it needed doing—feeding the dogs, answering the phone. A friend had a birthday and some people came over. I did what other people were doing: sucked in a hit of nitrous oxide, and, when the joint reached me on the sunken couch in my living room, I took a puff of synthetic pot (it was called Diablo, fittingly).

The next thing I remember, everything went blurry and I could see myself from above. I was floating out of my body into swirling colors, and it seemed like maybe this was my chance: I could leave the pain and shame of my life behind. The headaches and the heartbreak and the sense of failure—as a mother, a wife, and a woman—would just evaporate.

But there was still that question: *How did I get here?* After all the luck and success I'd had as an adult. After all the running I had to do to survive my childhood. After a marriage that started out feeling like magic, to the first person I ever really tried to show my whole self to. After I'd *finally* made peace with my body and stopped starving and torturing it—waging war on myself with food as the weapon. And, most importantly, after I'd raised three daughters and done everything I could think of to make myself the mother I never had. Did all of that struggle really add up to nothing?

Suddenly I was back in my body, convulsing on the floor, and I heard someone scream, "Call 911!"

I yelled "No!" because I knew what would come next: the ambulance, then the paparazzi, then *TMZ* announcing, "Demi Moore, rushed to the hospital on drugs!" And all of that happened, just like I knew it would. But something else happened that I didn't expect. I decided to sit still—after a life of running—and face myself. I'd done a lot in fifty years, but I don't know that I'd really *experienced* a lot, because I spent most of that time not quite there, afraid to be in myself, convinced I didn't deserve the good and frantically trying to fix the bad.

How did I get here? This is my story.

PART I
SURVIVAL

CHAPTER 1

It may sound strange, but I remember the time I spent in the hospital in Merced, California, when I was five years old as almost magical. Sitting up in bed in my soft pink fleecy nightgown waiting for my daily round of visitors—doctors, nurses, my parents—I felt completely comfortable. I'd already been there for two weeks and was determined to be the best patient they'd ever seen. There in the clean, bright room, everything felt like it was under control: there were dependable routines at the hospital enforced by real grown-ups. (In those days, there was a sense of awe around the doctors and nurses: everyone revered them, and to be in their midst felt like a privilege.) Everything made sense: I liked that there was a way I could behave that would yield predictable responses.

I had been diagnosed with kidney nephrosis, a life-threatening condition about which very little was known—it had really been studied only in boys, to the extent that it was studied at all. Basically, it's a retentive disease in which your filtering system isn't doing its job. I remember being terrified when my genitals swelled up and I showed my mom and saw her reaction: pure panic. She got me in the car and rushed me to the hospital, where I ended up staying for three months.

My aunt taught fourth grade, and she'd had her entire class make get-well cards, on construction paper with crayons and markers, which my parents delivered that afternoon. I was excited by the attention—from older kids, kids I didn't know. But when I looked up from the brightly colored cards, I saw my parents' faces. For the first time, I could feel their fear that I might not make it.

I reached over and touched my mother's hand and said, "Everything will be okay, Mommy."

She was just a kid, too. She was only twenty-three years old.

My mother, Virginia King, was a teenager who weighed a hundred pounds when she got pregnant with me just out of high school in Roswell, New Mexico. Really, she was a little girl. She labored in pain for nine hours, only to be knocked unconscious at the last minute, right before I came into this world. Not the ideal first attachment experience for either of us.

There was a part of her that did not really ground in reality, which meant that she was able to think outside the box. She came from poverty, but she didn't have a poverty mind-set— she didn't *think* poor. She wanted us to have the best: she would never have allowed a generic brand anything in our house—not cereal, not peanut butter, not laundry detergent. She was generous, expansive, welcoming. There was always room for one more person at the table. And she was confident in an easygoing kind of way—not a stickler for rules.

Growing up, I was aware that Ginny was different—she didn't seem like other moms. I can picture her in the car driving us to school, smoking a cigarette with one hand and putting her makeup on—perfectly—with the other, without even looking in the mirror. She had a great figure; she was athletic and had worked as a lifeguard at Bottomless Lakes State Park near Roswell. She was also strikingly attractive, with bright blue eyes, pale skin, and dark hair. She was meticulous about her appearance no matter what the circumstances: on our yearly trip to my grandmother's, she would make my dad stop three quarters of the way there so she could put in her curlers and have her hair just right by the time we got into town. (My mom went to beauty school, though she never turned it into a career.) She wasn't a fashion queen, but she knew how to put a look together with natural flair. She was always reaching for whatever was glamorous—she got my name from a beauty product.

She and my father made a magnetic pair, and they knew how to have fun; other couples flocked to them. My dad, Danny Guynes, who was less than a year older than my mom, always had a mischievous twinkle in his eye that made it seem like he had a secret you wanted in on. He had a beautiful mouth with bright white teeth offset by olive skin: he looked like a Latin

Tiger Woods. He was a charming gambler with a great sense of humor. Not boring. The kind of guy who is always riding the edge—always getting away with something. He was very macho, locked in competition with his twin brother, who was bigger and stronger and had joined the Marines, whereas my dad was rejected because he had a lazy eye, as I did. To me it was our special thing: I felt like it meant that we looked at the world the same way.

He and his twin were the oldest of nine children. His mother, who was from Puerto Rico, took care of me for a while when I was a baby. She died when I was two. His dad was Irish and Welsh, a cook for the Air Force, and a terrible alcoholic. He stayed with us when I was a toddler, and I have memories of my mother not wanting to leave me alone in the bathroom with him. Later, there was talk of sexual abuse. Like me, my dad was raised in a home full of secrets.

Danny graduated from Roswell High a year before Ginny, and when he left to go to college in Pennsylvania, she felt insecure—even more so when she found out he had a female "roommate." So she did what she would continue to do throughout their relationship whenever she felt a threat: she started seeing another guy to make him jealous. She took up with Charlie Harmon, a strapping young fireman whose family had moved to New Mexico from Texas. She even *married* him, though the union was short-lived, because the romance had the desired effect: Dad came running back. She divorced Charlie, and my parents got married in February 1962. I was born nine months later. Or so I thought.

WHEN PEOPLE HEAR "Roswell," they think of little green men, but nobody talked about UFOs at my house. The Roswell of my early childhood was a military town. We had the biggest landing strip in the United States (it served as a backup strip for the space shuttle) at Walker Air Force Base, which closed in the late sixties. Besides that, there were pecan orchards, alfalfa fields, a fireworks store, a meatpacking plant, and a Levi's factory. We were enmeshed in Roswell, very much a part of the fabric of the community. And our families were intertwined, so much so that my cousin DeAnna is also my aunt. (She is my mom's niece and married my dad's youngest brother.)

Mom had a much younger sister, Charlene—we called her Choc—who was a cheerleader at the high school. Ginny took on the role of chaperone, and I became the team's miniature mascot. She would do things like sneak the whole squad into the drive-in by letting them lie in a giggly pile in the trunk of her car. I felt like I was one of the big girls—in on their shenanigans. They would dress me up in a matching uniform, and Ginny would do my hair. At school assemblies, I was the big reveal: running out in my little powder-blue outfit to finish the cheer, complete with the signature move they taught me, the ceremonial flipping of the bird. It was my first taste of being a performer, and I reveled in every second of it. And I loved seeing how happy it made my mother.

In those days, my dad was working in advertising for the *Roswell Daily Record.* In the morning he would leave my mom a pack of cigarettes and a dollar bill, which she spent on a great big Pepsi that she bought from the corner store and nursed all day long. My dad was driven to succeed: he worked hard, and he played hard—sometimes too hard. He would go out carousing with one of my uncles, and they were the kind of drinkers who got into fights. (Keep in mind: they were barely twenty.) It was not uncommon for my dad to come home pretty banged up after one of these benders. He loved fighting, and he loved watching people fight. When I was little—way too little—my dad would take me to watch local boxing matches with him. I remember being about three and standing on top of a chair peering into the ring. I asked my dad, "What color trunks do I root for?" Watching two men pummeling each other: that was our bonding time.

Both my parents had what you might call a relaxed relationship with the truth, but I think Dad actually got joy out of feeling he could get one over on someone. He would go to pay a check, for example, and say to the guy at the cash register, "I'll flip you: double or nothing." It was the gambler in him, always looking to get away with whatever he could. I didn't have the words for it then, but his recklessness made me anxious. I was always on guard, on the alert for whether somebody was going to get angry. I have a vague memory of a man showing up at our house and pounding on the door when I was four, and of how terrified I was not knowing what was happening or why, but feeling the fear in my house. It was probably someone my dad had scammed. Or maybe he'd slept with the guy's wife.

I was almost five when my brother, Morgan, was born, and I felt protective of him right away. I was always tougher than him. He's a big guy now—six feet three inches and strong—but he was tiny as a kid, and so pretty people always assumed he was a girl. He was a fussy baby, and my mother indulged him: "Just give the baby what he wants!" was her singsong refrain. I remember on one very long drive to go visit my aunt in Toledo when Morgan was around two, my parents passed me a bottle of beer from the front seat, which I slowly administered to him all the way to our destination, the way you'd give a baby a bottle of milk. Needless to say, by the time we got out of the car, he wasn't screaming anymore.

I'm not saying I was the perfect sister: my nickname for Morgan was, after all, "Butthole." (One of my favorite forms of torture was to pin him down, fart into my hand, and hold it over his nose.) But I had a clear sense from early on that I had to look out for him—for both of us, really, because ours were not exactly helicopter parents. Once, when Morgan was three or four, he was standing on the back of the couch, looking out the window, and jumping, and I remember saying to my mother, "He's going to fall and hurt himself!" He did, of course, and I tried to catch him, but I was too small. I broke his fall, but

I couldn't stop him from cracking his head open on the coffee table. It was like a scene out of a movie: my mom jumping up and yelling, "Don't move!," and wrapping his bleeding head in a towel before we rushed him to the hospital. He had fractured his skull, and for a long time after they stitched him up he looked like Frankenstein's monster.

Soon after he was born we left Roswell for California, the first of a series of moves that would define our childhood. My mother figured out that my dad was having an affair, so she did what she'd been taught to do by her mother when your husband is fooling around: she got him away from "the problem." It did not seem to occur to the women in my family that if you took your cheating husband along when you left, the problem came with you wherever you went.

For most people, the idea of moving is a big deal. All that change; having to find a new place to live; the hassle and stress of setting up life and finding a new doctor and dry cleaner and grocery store—not to mention getting your kids settled in new schools and figuring out the school bus route and so on. It would require a lot of thought and preparation and planning.

That's not how it was for us. My brother and I have calculated that throughout our childhoods, we attended at least two new schools a year, and it was often more than that. I didn't realize until much later that this wasn't how everybody lived. When I hear about people who've had the same friends since kindergarten, I can't imagine what that must be like.

Moving wasn't dolled up for us kids. There would be a

mounting sense that something was going on, a plan was being hatched, and the next thing I knew we'd be hitting the road in one of the many earth-toned vehicles my parents had over the years: the rust-colored Maverick, the brown Pinto, the beige Ford Falcon. (They were all brand new, except for my dad's prized '55 baby-blue Chevy Bel Air.) It was often presented as a necessity: Dad was so good at what he did—and he *was* good at what he did—that they needed him at another paper in another town. Our job was to support him. In those early years, moving didn't feel like a big deal or a hardship. It was just what we did.

I WAS HOSPITALIZED for my kidneys a second time when I was eleven, and coincidentally or not, it was right after one of my father's affairs. Of course, at the time, I didn't know in any literal way that my dad was cheating, yet I can't help but wonder if my kidney flare-ups weren't my body's way of expressing what was going on at home. It was a Band-Aid, but for a while at least, it put the focus back on our family.

Ironically, at that point things had seemed unusually settled: we'd moved back to Roswell a few years earlier, and it had felt like coming home. We lived in a sweet three-bedroom ranch; I had my own room, with a pink canopy bed and a matching bedspread. Morgan shared his room with my dad's little brother George. (George had been living with us since I was five—as peripatetic as my parents were, they had taken him in without hesitation when my paternal grandmother died and he had no other place to go. He was like a big brother to me.) We'd made friends with the four kids who lived across the street, and we went back and forth between the two houses seamlessly—it was the first time we'd been in one place long enough for me to make friends I can really remember.

I was walking home from school one day when I felt a strange heat spreading through my body. The skin on my belly and my cheeks was getting tighter and tighter. I rushed to the bathroom and pulled down my pants to check my "cookie," but this time I was swelling up everywhere.

At St. Mary's Catholic Hospital in Roswell, I was surrounded by nuns. I quickly settled into the familiar routine: they had to measure my urine output and take my blood twice a day—it was before they invented those little plastic ports so they had to stick a new needle into my veins every single time. But even with all that poking and pricking, I felt at ease, knowing I was being taken care of.

By chance, Morgan had to get an operation for a hernia at the same time, and they put us together in one room. I was the expert on hospital life, and anyway, I was his big sister: as long as we were in that room, I was in charge. (We did argue about what to watch on television, though, and this was before remote controls, so to change the channel we needed to call in a nun. Morgan didn't care—he was six—but I was worried about losing my status as world's best patient. When he got better, I wasn't sad to see him go.)

When I went back to school, I still had to have my urine tested regularly, and I would get pulled out of class to go to the principal's office so they could make sure I had my snack. I was so bloated from steroids that a classmate asked me if I was Demi's sister. I didn't feel special the way I had at the hospital; I felt embarrassed and different. I didn't want people to see me like this.

And so I was almost relieved when my parents told us we were moving again. My mother, I would later discover, had found a red pubic hair in my father's underpants when she was doing the laundry, and after my parents battled it out they came to the inevitable conclusion that there was only one thing to do: move. Farther than usual this time, to the other side of the United States: Canonsburg, Pennsylvania.

This was a big deal. My parents sat us down and told us in advance, which raised the pitch of the whole thing. And this time we got an actual U-Haul. I remember filling it up with our beds, the green couch, my mother's ceramic partridges, and that coffee table Morgan had busted his head on. When we'd finished packing, we didn't think there was enough room for all of us in the cab. My mother was half kidding when she suggested I sit down on the passenger's-side floorboard, by her feet. I took her up on the offer. It was fun down there: I laid out a blanket and an airplane pillow and made my own little cave.

It was a very long drive, made longer by a blizzard that was so bad my dad had to pull over because he couldn't see the road. I was down by the heater, so it felt cozy and safe in my spot.

CANONSBURG WAS VERY different culturally from New Mexico or California. We were from a "y'all" family, and everyone in Canonsburg said "y'uns" instead. (My mom's accent was always strong, wherever we were; Morgan does a great impression of her asking for "a big ole Coke and a b'rito"—i.e., a *burrito*.) It was particularly hard for my brother, who was more introverted than I was and often got bullied. I was tougher, scrappier. My coping mechanism was to go into every new situation and immediately start operating like a detective: How does it work here? What are people into? Who are my potential allies? What should I be afraid of? Who holds power? And of course, the big one: How can I fit in? I would try to crack the code, figure out what I had to do, and master it. These skills would become essential later on.

We settled into a development of townhouses in a hilly area with a pond that froze over in wintertime, which meant we could go ice-skating. Morgan learned to ride a bike. I was eleven years old and loved gymnastics. I was also just on the verge of puberty. I was desperate for breasts: every night, I lay in my bed and actually prayed for them.

I wasn't a child anymore, but my mom insisted that we still needed a babysitter; she didn't trust me to look after Morgan by myself. The girl she hired was the older sister of one of my classmates—let's call her Corey—who happened to be much more developed and mature than I was. I sulked when Corey's sister came to babysit, not wanting anything to do with her. The next morning, Corey added to the indignity by announcing to the entire school bus, "I guess Demi still needs a babysitter."

I can still feel the hot flush of humiliation surging through my body. I was furious that my mother had put me in this position—had set me up like that. I remember feeling so exposed I thought I might die.

I wasn't going to let this define my stint at Canonsburg Elementary. I didn't need a babysitter. What I needed was a boyfriend.

I chose the cutest boy in the class: a blue-eyed, shaggy-haired blond named Ryder. And in a very short time, I was doing my victory lap, parading around the school holding his hand. Which actually felt really nice—for a moment.

WHILE I WAS dealing with the normal preteen girl stuff, my parents were coming undone. I'll never know what the catalyst was for their descent in Canonsburg, but things started to fall apart that spring.

One evening, as my dad was sitting in the kitchen making his way through his usual six-pack of Coors and listening to James Taylor, he decided to clean his gun. I remember the way he looked that night: when he drank, his lazy eye went even more askew, and everything about him seemed glazed over. He didn't notice there was a bullet in the chamber. When it went off, he blew a hole in the wall and the bullet grazed his forehead. There was blood everywhere. After the mess was cleaned up, my mother laughed it off, though inside I'm sure she was terrified. When I think about someone getting hammered and taking out a loaded gun in a house with kids running around, it's just beyond me.

Another night that spring, I woke up to the sound of distressed voices and commotion. I stumbled into my parents' room, where I found my mother thrashing and crying as my father struggled to hold her down. By the bed I saw a bottle of yellow pills. "Help me!" he screamed when he noticed me in their doorway. I walked toward them in a trance, not knowing—but on another level understanding completely—what I was witnessing: my mother trying to kill herself.

The next thing I remember is using my fingers, the small fingers of a child, to dig the pills my mother had tried to swallow out of her mouth while my father held it open and told me what to do. Something very deep inside me shifted then, and it never shifted back. My childhood was over. Any sense that I could count on either of my parents evaporated. In that moment, with my fingers in the mouth of my suicidal mother, who was flailing like a wild animal, and the sound of my father screaming directions at me, I moved from being someone who they at least *tried* to take care of to someone they expected to assist them in cleaning up their messes.

CHAPTER 2

It was the early seventies, and my mom did what people were starting to do: she went to a therapist. She was going to get help and get better. She was going to find herself! There was the ambient energy of the women's movement floating around the culture at that time, and we had a feminist neighbor my mother became friendly with who probably introduced Ginny to some of the ideas and catchphrases of women's liberation. But in her fragile state my mom was impressionable: after she saw *The Exorcist*, she went through a Charismatic Christianity phase. She would take me to services at a Catholic church where they played George Harrison songs and danced around in dashikis.

She was trying to figure out who she was. Sometimes I would "overhear" her talking with our neighbor at the kitchen table about how she was struggling. (I was such a snoop, my parents would joke that I "didn't want to miss a fart." But looking back, I see that what I was doing was patrolling for chaos. My mother had just tried to kill herself: I had to stay on high alert.) She would complain about the ways my dad didn't appreciate her and the deprivations of her childhood. They had been so poor that one Christmas she got her own doll wrapped up as a present, just wearing new clothes. To her, that doll symbolized the scarcity of her upbringing—the lack of money, nurturing, and attention she grew up craving. I heard that story many times.

I could feel the dynamics shift just a little in our house: for years, my mom had put up with my dad's cheating and had been completely dependent on him financially and emotionally. It's sad to say, but when she tried to kill herself, it had the effect of reclaiming a little power: she had shown my dad she might be capable of leaving him. Unfortunately, she had shown her children she was capable of leaving us, too.

My mother was repeating her own family history. Her first experience of male love was from the same kind of flirtatious, charismatic troublemaker as my dad. My maternal grandfather, Bill King, didn't think much of my dad when my mother first started going out with him in high school, but the two men had a lot in common. Granddaddy was a charming womanizer and rule bender who played stand-up bass in a country band. He was very tough: one time when he had a toothache and they didn't have the money for a dentist, he went up to the bathroom with a razor blade and cut the tooth out himself. Eventually, Granddaddy had a wild death to match his wild life: he was out drinking one night when he drove his beloved blue El Camino into—and under—a moving truck. He was decapitated.

I was ten when he died. I remember him as a silver fox, handsome and rugged, his strong hands stained by motor oil. He owned a little gas station where my cousins and I loved to play, but when my mom was young, he was out of work for a long time after he broke his back on the job, working construction with a road crew. My grandmother had to support them and the three daughters they had at the time—my mom and her older sisters, Billie and Carolyn. This was distinctly not the life my grandma Marie had hoped for. She had her heart set on going to college. Growing up on the border of Texas and New Mexico in a strict Pentecostal home, she was the first member of her family to graduate high school. But Marie ended up a young wife and mother working full time to make ends meet. She was stretched thin.

My mother's interpretation of my grandma's unavailability was that she, Ginny, was unlovable. She was a skinny, sickly child, and she never got over feeling neglected—never enough money, never enough love, an afterthought. It never occurred to her that my grandmother simply didn't have the bandwidth to nurture her the way she might have wanted. Ginny wasn't able to put herself in my grandmother's shoes and imagine what it was like for *her* as a young woman, living with a cheating husband for whom she'd given up her dreams, having to support a family without the benefit of training or education—and taking care of three little kids on top of that.

My grandma Marie was by far the most dependable grown-up in

my life. She was raised on a broomcorn farm in Elida, New Mexico, in the 1930s, and possessed a practical farmer's do-what-needs-to-be-done competence. She was solid, consistent, and trustworthy. But for all her good qualities, she had taught my mother—who in turn taught me—some strange coping mechanisms. Whenever Granddaddy was unfaithful, he would convince Grandma Marie that it was the *women* who were the problem. He persuaded her after one affair that they had to move to get away from his pursuer, so they picked up and left for Richmond, California, where my mother was born. When Ginny was about twelve, after they'd moved back to Roswell, she came home early from school one day and walked in on her father in bed with his brother's wife. His reaction was to scream at my mom—blame his daughter for the situation. He had been my mother's safe harbor; she worshipped him. Their relationship was never the same after that.

ONE HOT SUMMER afternoon in Canonsburg, Ginny told me giddily that I should hurry and get packed; we were going to a hotel. It didn't make any sense, but I got caught up in my mother's enthusiasm as she hustled Morgan and me into her Pinto and took us to a nearby hotel with lots of blond wood, where everything was brightly lit and sparkling clean. My excitement fizzled into confusion and anxiety when she told us that we would be staying there because she was leaving Dad for her shrink, Roger. They were in love, she explained; Roger was paying for the room, and we would be moving with him to California, where he was going to build a glass house for us to live in. She even showed us the plans.

It was a solid sales pitch. She presented her new plan as perfectly reasonable and already settled, with no acknowledgment that her kids might experience some pain or fear or confusion about their parents splitting up. Partly, this was because she was too caught up in her fantasy to consider our feelings, but I also wonder if, at some level, she knew this was nowhere near the end of her relationship with my dad.

Roger was a tall, sandy-haired guy with blue eyes and wire-rimmed glasses who had grown up in Northern California. Clearly, he was not a therapist who subscribed to a professional code of ethics. It's heartbreaking when you consider that my mother went to him trying to find help: she saw him as the answer to all her problems, a sober, educated man who could put her on a different path. Instead, she found one more guy to complicate her life. He prescribed her uppers and downers, and I doubt she was following the recommended dosage. The pills, along with the alcohol she drank to wash them down, made her more unpredictable than ever.

My parents started going through the motions of splitting up. My mother moved in with Roger, and we alternated between staying with her at the hotel and with my dad at the apartment. A few weeks later, he told us we were going on a road trip. Off we went to Ohio, to visit my aunt and uncle in Toledo. Only he didn't tell my mom. From her perspective, we had all just vanished. (I can only imagine the powerlessness and raw panic she must have felt.) Dad told our relatives that she had abandoned us for Roger without a word, that he had no idea how to reach her, and they believed him. Morgan and I were so accustomed to things not adding up that I don't know if we even bothered to question the situation, or wonder why Ginny wasn't calling and checking in on us. In any case, we were distracted: my aunt and uncle took us with their kids on a road trip to the Grand Ole Opry in Nashville. For me the main attraction was Minnie Pearl, who had, always, a price tag dangling from her hat.

None of this would fly now, of course, in the age of cell phones, Instagram, email, and FaceTime, but it was easy to disappear in the seventies. My dad had made it something of a specialty. When we were in one place long enough for bills to start showing up at the door, he would write "deceased" next to his name on the envelope and take it back to the post office. I remember a microwave he bought from Sears—when microwaves seemed like a miraculous invention—that he made Morgan sign for when the deliveryman brought it to our house. My dad then told Sears he wouldn't pay for it because a child's signature wasn't legally binding. He stiffed stores for all kinds of things with schemes like that; he was a creative guy. If either one of my parents had ever applied their intelligence to something constructive, I honestly believe they could have been highly successful. They had the brains, they just didn't have the tools to pursue a positive path. And so much of their energy was focused on self-sabotage, or on sabotaging each other—I think we treat the people we love the way we believe, in our deepest hearts, that we deserve to be treated ourselves.

That summer in Toledo, my dad had no idea how to be alone with us. I had always felt connected to him, but he was so withdrawn by this point that it was impossible to feel close. He loved us, sure. But he hadn't kidnapped us because he was determined to spend quality time with his children or because he was genuinely afraid Ginny would take us to California and he'd never see us again. I think our time in Ohio was just one extended power play in my parents' never-ending love-hate struggle—and I suppose he won that particular round. Because somehow, by the end of the summer, he'd convinced my mom to forgive him for kidnapping her children, and we headed back to Pennsylvania so they could give it another shot.

Everything was going to be different. We were—of course—going to move, to a bigger house in another town in Pennsylvania called Charleroi, thirty miles outside of Pittsburgh. It was a step up on every level. A spacious, modern house painted avocado green, with high ceilings and shiny new appliances that my mother loved. The plumbing needed work, but Dad was good at that: he blew cigarette smoke through the pipes and had Morgan sit up in the bathroom and yell down to tell him which was the hot tap and which was the cold based on where the smoke came out.

Of all the places we lived, I think that house most closely matched my mom's fantasy of what life should look like. Unlike her mother, Ginny's aspirations early on were conventional: she wanted to be a beautiful wife and mother who was adored by her husband and had a nice home. And she *had* made nice homes for us, everywhere we went. She had a knack for decorating; she managed to whip each house we lived in into shape almost as soon as we got there: sewing curtains, arranging the furniture and knickknacks she got from a company called Home Interiors, and generally making things look lived in, as if we'd been there for years. But at the Green House, as my brother and I called it, she outdid herself. That house was the embodiment of her domestic ambitions. I was even allowed to get a puppy. Unfortunately, it went to the bathroom in front of my dad's closet and he gave me a "spanking" for that with his belt. (I didn't cry, though. I never, ever cried, no matter what.) The puppy went back.

Of course, nothing was really different in Charleroi. The same stuff was just happening in a different house. Danny was gambling and drinking to excess. He was an excellent pool player, and, when he was lucky, he would convince some unsuspecting fool to bet against him, saying that he could win with one eye covered. Then Danny would cover up the lazy eye he could barely see out of anyway, and proceed to rake in the other guy's money.

It didn't always go his way. He lost huge amounts of money playing poker and would come home raging, drunk, and broke. At one point my father turned to a mafia loan shark to cover his gambling losses, and he was indebted to the mob for years afterward. He had already been working with them to sway local elections for mafia-favored candidates and other low-level, unsavory stuff like that. However indirect my dad's involvement, it was still dangerous. He got into a shoot-out outside of a bar in Charleroi once. Another time, my mom went with a female friend to a pub in town and was spotted by a mobster who called my dad: he told my dad that mob women weren't supposed to be out unaccompanied like that; it didn't look right.

I, meanwhile, started seventh grade, which in Charleroi was part of the giant, terrifying high school. As always, I was the new girl. It's possible that all the adapting I had to do primed me to become an actress: it was my job to portray whatever character I thought would be most popular in every new school, in every new town. I identified the in crowd and studied them for clues: Did the cool girls wear bell-bottoms or hot pants? What were their accents like? What did I need to do to be accepted? Was it best to try to stand out or blend in? It would be decades before it occurred to me that I could just be whoever I truly am, not the person I guessed other people wanted to see.

Needless to say, whenever I started to get a sense of a place, to decipher how I might fit in through sports or the social scene or what classes I might be good at, it was time to pick up and leave. Usually without much warning, or any kind of logical plan.

I DON'T KNOW which of my dad's illicit activities provoked this particular fight—whether it was another infidelity, or if he just got too nasty when he was drunk—but one afternoon when I was doing my homework to the background music of my parents fighting at the top of their lungs, I heard my mother scream, "I've had it with your shit!" She came storming into my room and told Morgan and me to grab our stuff and get in the car, we were going back to Roswell.

This was nothing out of the ordinary, of course: we were pretty efficient at packing by this point, and we were used to hitting the road for hours on end while my mother chain-smoked out the window. But going back to Roswell was a departure from the exhausting routine of starting over from scratch. Insofar as we understood the concept, Roswell was home. It was where we came from, where we had family and history and an understanding of the culture and the community. And then there was Grandma Marie, whom I'd called "Mother" as a little girl, and who was, in many ways, the only adult I really trusted. Staying with her was grounding, soothing. When we got to her house, it was a relief just to be in her midst.

Even with half a dozen states between them, my parents managed to keep their drama explosive. The screaming phone calls began almost as soon as we arrived—my father's voice was so loud through the receiver it felt like he was there in the room. My mother would stalk around the house sobbing histrionically, while I tried to stay out of her way. Morgan escaped into his projects: taking apart and putting back together the vacuum cleaner motor, disassembling the alarm clock to see how it worked. When my aunts came around, I realized they were shooting knowing glances at each other during my mother's outbursts and drinking binges. For the first time I felt embarrassed by her. And I was ashamed of myself for feeling that way.

Ginny wanted me to take her side and tell everyone how horrible my dad had been to her, but I couldn't. Aside from the gambling, I felt they were equally to blame for the chaos in our lives. Now that I was old enough, I could see how childish she was compared to her sisters—how rarely she took responsibility for herself, and how her default mode was to blame everyone else: my dad, my grandmother, whoever. Little by little, I started to wall myself off from her. With my grandmother around, I didn't need to overlook my mother's craziness just to survive.

So, on the inevitable afternoon when Ginny said we were going back to my dad, I didn't get up and start packing as I always had in the past. Dad had gotten a new job in Washington State, north of Seattle, Ginny told me and my grandmother, and the plan was to return to him in Pennsylvania and then move to the other side of the country together as a family.

I looked at my grandmother. I looked at my mom. And then I said, "I'm not going." Ginny didn't give me a good enough reason for returning to the man she'd been spending all of her waking hours maligning to her family or fighting with on the phone. I was sick of things not adding up. Whatever it was they were doing, I didn't want to be a part of it. My mother tried to persuade me, but she saw that I was immovable. She took Morgan and went back to Charleroi without me.

That summer, I did gymnastics at the Y, where I made my

first best friend, Stacy Welch. My grandmother enrolled me in the better public school in Roswell in the fall—we weren't zoned for it, but Grandma Marie finagled it by dropping me off every morning at Stacy's house, and then Stacy and I would walk to the bus or Mrs. Welch would drive us to school. I made the cheerleading squad. Suddenly, I was living like a normal person, like everybody else. It felt great.

Once Ginny made it to Washington with my brother, I started getting the push: "You should come up here; it's beautiful, you'd love it!" And there was a part of me that felt *you should be with your parents*—a dutiful pull. But why? I was doing fine.

My grandmother took care of me with a consistency I'd never before experienced. She made sure that I finished my homework, brushed my teeth, got to bed on time. She let me paint my room bright yellow because I loved Tweety Bird so much. She was attentive to everything in my life, including the friends I was making at school. If I went to the movies, she would pick me up, or, if she was working, she'd arrange to have someone else get me. Never once was I left standing on a street corner, wondering if anyone would show up. The daily disasters of life with my parents were nonexistent. In essence, I got the version of my grandmother that my mother had always yearned for.

After my granddaddy died, my grandmother went through a prolonged mourning period. For almost two years, every day when she got home from her job in the office of a legal title company, she lay on the couch in the living room without turning on the lights. Then she met a lovely guy named Harold and found love again. They had their regular schedule, and I became part of their routines: Tuesday and Saturday nights they went dancing, so I either had a sleepover at a friend's house or someone came and slept over with me. Wednesday was Grandma Marie's standing appointment at the beauty parlor, and when she finished getting her hair done after work, we would go out to dinner, just the two of us, at one of the usual spots: the Mexican restaurant, Furr's cafeteria, or the Chinese place. The Roswell rotation.

It was a halcyon period of safety, a time when I saw what a parent could be—should be—and an example I would look to when I became a mother. And yet, I started to get restless. By that point, I was conditioned to not stay in one place for too long. I didn't have any experience in following through; I had no barometer for the hardships—or the rewards—of commitment. I've often wondered what my life would be like if I'd remained in Roswell. I would have had to work on developing and maintaining friendships, which had always been disposable. I would have had to set goals for myself, which I'd never done, because we weren't in one place long enough to see them through.

None of that happened. I had learned to crave extremes: it was like I needed the juice of it. I lasted six months in Roswell. Then I went back to my parents.

CHAPTER 3

I was with my family in Washington for just two months before they decided we were moving, this time to Southern California—and in a hurry. Maybe it was because of a mistress, maybe they were dodging a bill collector, or maybe the Pacific Northwest chapter of the mafia had figured out where to find my dad. We may simply have been evading Roger the therapist. My mother had stolen his credit card, and we used it to pay for our trip to California.

Somewhere along the never-ending nineteen-hour drive to Redondo Beach, my dad got badly beaten up; his face was swollen and bruised and he had a black eye. He looked awful: I can picture his battered face behind the wheel. In keeping with the silence that surrounded every unpleasant aspect of my family's life, there was no explanation or discussion.

Once we were installed in our new place in Redondo

Beach—an apartment in a beachy, stucco, pseudo-hacienda-style complex a mile from the water—my mother told me that when anyone called I should say that both my parents were away and couldn't be reached. They were eluding the phone company, the electric company, and credit card carriers—all of whom would ask to speak to the variations of my parents' names they'd been given, like "Virginia King," my mother's maiden name, or my dad's first and middle names, "Danny Gene." My parents even rented our apartment under the names of my aunt DeAnna and my uncle George, my father's little brother, who lived nearby in L.A.

This came to light when George and DeAnna decided to move into our apartment complex and discovered that, thanks to my parents, they were already there. I don't even remember them being particularly angry about it; they simply assumed my parents' names for the purposes of their own lease. Having my aunt and uncle so close by was a huge comfort. As my mom and dad spiraled further out of control, George and DeAnna filled in the gaps time after time: they gave us rides when we needed them, fed us, listened to us when we had problems. They took me to my first concert: Aerosmith, in 1975. (They wanted to sit up in the stands; my friend and I were desperate to get onto the grass down where the action was. During "Sweet Emotion," I remember, a stranger casually passed me a bottle of rum; I went to lift it to my mouth, but DeAnna snatched it away.)

Southern California in the mid-seventies was different from anywhere we'd been before. I was in seventh grade—at my third school that year—and all the cool kids wore Dittos jeans and smoked cigarettes and pot. I became close with a girl named Adrien, who had long blond hair: the quintessential California girl in a tube top. She was my mentor in misbehaving, introducing me to hard liquor and Marlboro Reds.

I got busted smoking at school and was sent to the principal's office. My punishment was suspension. I was horrified. I'd never been in trouble before; up until then fitting in had never required acting out. My mom came to pick me up, and we were quiet on the way home. Then she removed a cigarette from her pack, waved it in my direction, and said, "Go ahead." Instead, I took out one of my own. She reached over and lit it, and we never talked about it again.

That marked the beginning of a new stage in our relationship. I was only thirteen, but when I asked Ginny if I could go with friends to a club in the Valley, she said, "Sure—take the car. If you get stopped by the police just say you're driving it without your parents' permission." I had learned how to drive back in Roswell, but I didn't know the Valley. I didn't know the freeway. I had no experience driving at night. Somehow, I made it to the club, with two other kids—who are lucky to be alive—as my passengers. From then on, I was regularly assigned to run family errands in that car. "Just remember: we don't know you're driving it," Ginny told me. It was convenient for my parents, and it was one more way of seeing what they could get away with.

My parents didn't set boundaries for me because they couldn't even set them for themselves. They were drinking more than ever and taking Percodan, Valium, and Quaaludes that my father somehow obtained prescriptions for and filled at different drugstores using all my parents' various aliases. He had the look to go with the partying: bell-bottoms and long sideburns. He even got a perm.

As for my mother, she often got aggressive when she mixed drugs and alcohol, and my parents got kicked out of restaurants and bars as a matter of course. My mom would start a fight with other patrons or lose her temper with my dad and start breaking dishes. Once, when she didn't like the way the check was delivered, she took off her high-heeled shoe and used it as a weapon against the waitress.

Somehow, in the middle of all their partying, my mom found a good job as a bookkeeper for a magazine distribution company owned by a man named Frank Diskin. DeAnna started working for him, too, and suddenly my family had more money—especially my mother. Frank gave her luxurious bonuses: a mink coat and, eventually, the ultimate status symbol for a New Mexico girl of that era, a Cadillac Seville in pale yellow. We ended up moving into the nicest house we'd ever occupied in Marina del Rey, with Frank Diskin paying our rent.

Why was this guy willing to spend so much on his bookkeeper?

DeAnna remembers that whenever my mother was alone with Frank in his office, the door was always locked.

EVER SINCE THE episode in Canonsburg when my mother had tried to kill herself, I'd been subconsciously waiting for another disaster—another truly devastating situation that didn't make sense, that I couldn't control, and that would upend my already unstable life. It arrived without warning when I came home from school one day to find that my brother, my father, and almost every trace of them had vanished. "Where's Morgan?" I asked my mother. "Where's Dad?" It was not unprecedented for my dad to go missing, but my brother? She shrugged. "Your father and I are getting a divorce," she said. "And he'd only consent if I gave him Morgan."

I was stunned. I don't know what was worst: losing my brother, losing my dad, or finding out that my father couldn't bear to be parted from Morgan but was fine with abandoning me.

"You and I are moving to West Hollywood," Ginny informed me. "I've found an apartment on Kings Road." Frank Diskin was out of the picture. As my mother and DeAnna told it, the IRS had been after my father for back taxes for years, and when they caught up with him, he gave them dirt on Diskin in exchange for his own freedom. Basically, he offered the government the same deal he'd offered so many others: double or nothing.

There was only one problem. Losing Diskin meant losing our relative prosperity. Both my mother and DeAnna were out of jobs, and my family wouldn't be able to stay in the house in the Marina. My mother was furious, and I guess for her it was the final straw that convinced her she'd be better off without my dad. Evidently, my father had hit a breaking point, too: before he left, he'd cut Ginny's beautiful mink coat into pieces.

I was still reeling when she took me to see our new neighborhood. She was on a manic high, pointing out all the bars and movie theaters, the shops and restaurants. The complex where we were going to live was massive, but the actual apartment was tiny: one bedroom, which we would share; a kitchenette; and a little balcony overlooking the pool. It was like everything in my life was shrinking: my home, my family.

NOW THAT IT was just the two of us, my dynamic with Ginny shifted. It was more like we were sisters than mother and daughter. I was already used to living without rules or limits, but now we even started to *look* more like peers. I was developing into a teenager; and Ginny basically dressed like one, in miniskirts and low-cut tops. She dolled herself up every time she went out the apartment door. She had deliberately chosen a building where there were other single people and divorcées, and she made friends with one of our neighbors, Landi, who would go with her to the bars.

From our balcony, I used to see this beautiful girl hanging out at the pool, swimming and lying in the sun, growing ever more golden. She was the most radiant creature I'd ever seen, a German actress a few years older than I was, named Nastassja Kinski. I became her friend and acolyte.

The director Roman Polanski had brought Nastassja and her mother to America so that Nastassja could improve her English and her accent at Lee Strasberg's acting studio. Polanski wanted Nastassja to star in *Tess*, a romantic tragedy he was going to make based on the Thomas Hardy novel, and he was willing to put off the film until she was ready. That's how much faith he had in her, which certainly made sense to me. As far as I could tell, she was perfect.

She was self-possessed and *in her body* like nobody I'd ever seen before. She owned her sexuality completely, without self-consciousness or discomfort, with complete confidence and ease. In my whole life, I haven't met many who have that in the way that she did. Nastassja was only seventeen, but she had already been in four films. Her star was on the rise in Hollywood, and she regularly received scripts from directors who wanted to work with her. That's where I came in. Nastassja could speak English well, but she couldn't really read it, so she asked me to read the screenplays out loud to her so she could decide which ones she wanted to pursue.

She would stare at me with her enormous green eyes, listening intently, and by the time I finished reading her a script, she'd know exactly what she thought; she had total clarity in her opinions. I was as dazzled by her confidence and her sense of direction as I was by her beauty and sensuality. And I saw the breathtaking effect that combination had on other people: like me, they were overcome by her sense of comfort, freedom, and power—though I doubt I identified it as power at the time, as the concept was unimaginable to me. I didn't know what it was that she had, but I wanted it for myself.

Nastassja's mom may have been even less reliable than mine. It had fallen to Nastassja, from the age of *twelve*, to support them both. I wasn't paying for my mother's life (yet), but I understood the feeling of being responsible for the person who was supposed to be responsible for you. Emotionally, it felt like it was my job to keep Ginny alive. It was a sad but powerful thing Nastassja and I had in common. For a time, we were very close.

I decided to follow Nastassja's example—I wanted to do what she did, and if that meant acting, then so be it. I learned by watching, observing, asking myself: *How is this person doing this? What do you need to do to make this work—do you need to get an agent?* (Not: *I want to be an actor,* mind you. But: *How do I make this happen?*) I went with Nastassja to her dance classes, trying to emulate her grace, and one night she took me along to dinner with Polanski. He tracked me down to invite me to dinner a second time months later, and I went with my mom. He was a perfect gentleman on both of those evenings, but he had been convicted of having sex with a thirteen-year-old girl. (I saw this dynamic all around me. Thirteen was a little extreme, but in my world, believe it or not, relationships with underage girls was the norm.) He expected probation following his plea bargain, but the judge saw it differently. Faced with imprisonment, Polanski fled the United States just a few days after that second dinner. He ended up making *Tess* in France; the film received three Oscars, and Nastassja won a Golden Globe.

I was disappointed when she moved out of the apartment building. It would be two decades before we saw each other again—unexpectedly, at Elizabeth Taylor's regular Sunday lunch. When we embraced, it was like a homecoming. We knew each other in a way that no one else could.

MY DAD WAS living with Morgan in Redondo Beach, and we went to visit them—he wouldn't let Morgan come to our place. Ginny was behind the wheel in the yellow Cadillac she had managed to hang on to from Diskin, with Landi along for the ride in back. I sat in the passenger seat, explaining to Landi the complicated history of my parents' relationship, which I had put together from years of snooping around. For instance, I knew from poking through the metal fireproof box where documents were stored that my birth certificate was dated November 11, 1962, and that the date on my parents' marriage license was February 1963—which at first I had assumed was a mistake: it should have said February 1962, nine months before I was born. But I'd since realized that they don't make mistakes on that kind of thing. Obviously, it took Ginny a while to get divorced from that guy Charlie she was with when my dad went to college, so she could marry my dad, who got her pregnant with me, and . . .

I stopped. I turned toward my mother. And out of my mouth came the words, "Is he my real father?" Somewhere deep down, though, I already knew the answer.

She snapped, "Who told you that?" But nobody told me. Nobody had to.

A flood of questions came into my head. *Who else knows about this?* Everybody, as it turned out: all my cousins, even the younger ones, knew that Danny was not my biological father. I thought of all the times I'd told them about the ways I was like him, how I inherited my eye problems from him, my love of spicy food, and they had stood there, looking at me, knowing I was clueless, deluded. *Why wasn't I ever told?* "Because your dad never wanted you to know," Ginny said. "He made everyone promise because he thought you wouldn't feel the same about him."

Ten minutes later, we were at my dad's impersonal stucco two-bedroom apartment. My mother dropped the bomb the second we walked in the door: "Demi knows." In no time, she had a drink in one hand and a cigarette in the other, and she seemed high on the drama of the situation—the power it had given her to hurt him.

He avoided meeting my eyes. He looked numb. It was only one in the afternoon, but he had likely polished off a six-pack before we got there.

Nobody asked me if I was okay, or if I had questions. Neither of my parents seemed to care about what this revelation meant to me.

They went into the bedroom and kept fighting, or maybe they started having sex . . . with them there was always a fine line.

I felt exposed and stupid and somehow dirty. So I did what they'd taught me to do when the shit hit the fan. I got in the car and took off. Not for good—yet. I had nowhere to go but back to my mother's apartment. But I was practicing.

CHAPTER 4

Not long after the bombshell dropped, I was visiting my aunt Choc in Amarillo, Texas. I told her that I knew about my dad. "It's about time," she said. She'd always liked my biological father, Charlie, she told me, and had happy memories from the time she spent with him and my mother. "You know, he lives in Texas," she added. "We could try calling him." She did, and the next day he showed up at her door. I didn't know what to feel or how to behave: he was a stranger, but he was my father. He was handsome, about five-ten, with brown hair, probably around thirty-five years old at the time. I looked to see where I might connect. In fact, my eye problem *was* something I'd inherited from my father—*this* father. He had been devastated, he told me, when my mom left him, and he had always wanted to meet me.

I was fourteen, and I wasn't equipped to cope with this situation. And it only got worse: Ginny showed up. Never content to let drama unfold without her at its center, she got on a plane the second Choc told her that Charlie was coming. When she arrived, she whisked Charlie off into a room alone. I spent the entire day compulsively rolling joints and smoking them, acting like I was just fine and didn't need a thing.

Charlie, on the other hand, was excited, and invited me to come and visit him and meet my grandparents and half siblings. A few months later, I flew to Houston and he picked me up at the airport—with his mistress. He dropped her off on the way to see his parents, who were so happy to meet me; they'd always wanted to, they said. As it turned out, my grandma Marie had snuck them a few photos over the years, knowing how much it would mean to them. I stayed with them that night.

Charlie's wife felt insecure—and rightfully so: he'd introduced me to his mistress first—and was reluctant to meet me. I went over to his house on my second day to meet her and my half siblings—one of whom was a brother from yet another one of Charlie's marriages who looked exactly like a male version of me. It was awkward. I didn't know where I fit in or even why I was there. I left feeling clear about one thing: Charlie may have been my biological father, but Danny was my dad.

The justification for having kept my paternity a secret from me was that Danny feared that if I found out, I would feel differently about him. But the reality was that once I knew, *he* pulled away from *me*. Even before my parents' split, he had become distant, withdrawing into drinking and drugs. And, of course, once they decided to divorce, it was my brother he couldn't live without, not me. But after my discovery, our relationship completely deteriorated. He ceased making any effort to see me; he stopped calling; when we did see each other—when my mom and I visited Morgan—he barely looked at me and his hugs were awkward and forced. He was just . . . gone.

DISCOVERING THAT I'D been lied to my entire life about something so profound wasn't great for my relationship with my mother, either. Whatever fragile trust we had shared was shattered now that I realized she had gotten pregnant with me when she was still with Charlie, and then just come up with a lie that was more convenient than the truth. But like every child in history who has been let down time and again by her parents, I held out the irrational hope that my mother would change and become someone I could count on.

Instead, one afternoon when I came home from school, I found her sprawled across the bed, surrounded by empty pill bottles. I remember calling the hospital for an ambulance in a kind of frozen trance, a dissociated state that would become increasingly familiar to me as years passed, in which I would leave my body and just *cope* without really being present. An ambulance came and took us to the hospital to get her stomach pumped. Everyone in the building saw the arrival of the paramedics and her departure from the apartment on a gurney. I was somehow simultaneously embarrassed, numb, and terrified.

My mother survived that incident. But her faux suicide attempts became a regular occurrence, a routine. Back would come the emergency medical teams with their sirens and gurneys, and off we'd go to get her stomach pumped again. She didn't want to die: she was crying out for help, and she wanted attention. Often, her overdoses followed some sort of devastating interaction with my dad. The man I thought of as my dad, anyway.

I was in a constant state of anxious vigilance. I never knew what I'd find when I walked through that apartment door: my mother's self-destructiveness was boundless, narcissistic, and unstoppable. And yet I was developing armor: I took comfort in my ability to deal with her crises and the knowledge that I could handle whatever came my way. I never felt I was going to fall apart, never turned to anybody and said, "I can't take this." I could get through anything she threw at me: if she tried to kill herself; if I had to peel her off of a bar stool; if she told me Danny wasn't my real dad. I would survive, no matter what. But I would survive by being on guard. And then, when crisis struck, by exiting my body: functional but frozen.

Everyone knew about my mother in our apartment complex, of course, and I adopted an invulnerable, self-sufficient persona in response. My character was on her own, unfettered by curfews or rules. Every time I tossed off "My mother doesn't care if I . . ." or "I can do whatever I want . . .," I rode the wave of that dubious freedom, but I also felt the emptiness of it. I did not feel particularly sympathetic toward Ginny. Even as a fourteen-year-old I realized that her self-absorption and "suicide attempts" came at my expense.

Her accelerating self-destructiveness lent an urgency to my attempts to define myself in opposition to her. *I'm a different person*, I kept telling myself. *I'm not like that.* But the insecurity that had been nipping at my heels was intensifying.

I was the girl whose mother was always trying to kill herself. I was the girl who'd been abandoned by *two* fathers. My wandering eye suddenly seemed like an obvious physical manifestation of the truth about me: I was just *off*, and everyone could tell. I had surgery just before I turned fifteen that finally fixed my eye, but in my own mind, I remained marked as broken.

All of this coincided with puberty. My transformation from a skinny, lazy-eyed kid to a young woman who men desired was confusing. The unfurling of my sexuality was linked for me on the deepest level with shame. It would be decades before I could even begin to disentangle the two.

I STARTED SPENDING time with a couple of guys who lived down the hall and were very friendly to me. They were older, in their mid- to late twenties, but I thought I could impress them and join their crowd by acting cooler and more mature than I actually was. I was alone a lot in my mother's apartment, and sometimes they'd stop by to visit, or I'd wander down the hall and hang out with them at their place.

One evening, I was in their apartment drinking beer, and we were all flirting. It was fun at first: I was still quite innocent, just beginning to discover the effect I had on guys. But I wasn't in any way prepared for the consequences. One of them made a move, and the other one disappeared. That was evidently what he had wanted from me all along, and somehow, I felt I had no choice, that it was my job to give it to him—like I was obligated to fulfill his expectation just because he harbored it. I blamed myself for acting provocative and older than my years.

Afterward, I was left with the hollow, empty feeling of being used. A new kind of lonely.

GINNY WAS NOT really interested in how I was doing at my vast new school, Fairfax High, and she didn't care about my report card or even seem to register that such a thing existed. When we spent time together, it was as if we were a pair of girlfriends out on the town. She never offered me any guidance; there was no talk about college, for example, or discussion of my future. Instead, the conversation revolved around how unfairly life had treated her, what she had missed out on, and how she wanted to find the kind of relationship she deserved.

She succeeded for a while when she took up with a great guy named Ron Felicia, who owned a recording studio. They actually had a seemingly healthy relationship, and he really grounded her for the short time they were together. For a few months, we even moved in with him. I didn't have to change schools, though I wouldn't have minded—I wasn't really involved in anything at Fairfax High. By that point, I was numb to the whole high school scene and was just trying to get through it. I'd managed to make few friends out of the thousand kids who were my classmates. (I'm sorry not to have crossed paths with Flea or Anthony Kiedis, who were at Fairfax at that time but whom I didn't befriend until decades later—though I seriously doubt I was cool enough to run with their crowd.)

Through Ron, I met a guy who was kind of a pretty-girl-type agent. It was difficult to get work because I was inexperienced and underage: Helen Hunt, Jodie Foster—people like that had all been acting since they were very young. I was on the outside looking in at the entertainment industry, and as I had always done, I learned by the fake-it-till-you-make-it method. I'd love to say that the underlying drive came from a fascination with plays that I encountered in school, or from the thrill of performing classic roles in drama class. I wish that was how I came to acting, but, in truth, Hollywood was like one more school I had to figure out, one more system to game. I chipped away at it, trying to grasp how it worked. It would be years before I made a living as an actress, but that first agent did get me a small role on a TV show called *Kaz* playing a thirteen-year-old prostitute. My big first line that got me my SAG card was, "Fifty dollars, mister."

As much as my mother wanted a relationship with a kind man, and Ron Felicia was that, she couldn't sustain it. Instead, she felt compelled to ruin it and managed to—dramatically— when Ron came home one day to find her in bed with my dad. Ron was understandably furious, punched Danny, and threw my mother out. She and I hastily moved to a little studio in Brentwood right off Sunset—I drive by it all the time, and I always feel a little pit in my stomach.

There were always men. Ginny and I got a lot of attention from them when we went out together at night. I remember sitting at the bar at Carlos 'n Charlie's, a trendy Mexican restaurant in West Hollywood. She was drinking too much and eyeing the guys at the bar flirtatiously. Whenever I recognized her boozy, blowsy come-hither look setting in I cringed. One of the men took the bait and came over to us. "Are you two sisters?" he asked. (It was Ginny's favorite question.) "No." She grinned. "This is my daughter." The man protested that she couldn't possibly be old enough to be my mother. And really, she wasn't: she was a thirty-four-year-old woman with a fifteen-year-old daughter. She chuckled as he leered at me.

I was beginning to resent my role as her bar companion; it seemed like she was just using me as bait for these men—and as her designated driver, albeit one without a license.

When I look back, it's incredible that we never got caught, but then again, in those days Ginny could have taught a master class at defying expectations (and odds). For somebody who was getting by on a thread, all the apartments we moved into, though small, were clean, often newly built, and generally in safe neighborhoods. We were never "slumming it." Maybe she was continuing the game she and my father used to play, staying one jump ahead of the landlords by using aliases, but whatever the reason, in the first two years after my parents split, we moved seven times. One move was a matter of safety, after a guy she'd been dating got angry at her: I came home from school one day to find all the electrical wires cut and the smell of urine in our apartment. He'd come by and marked every corner of the place, like a dog.

The stress of being on the run from apartment to apartment was contributing, I'm sure, to my mother's instability as well as my own anxiety. One night when I came home late, she was waiting by the door. "Where have you been? You know you're supposed to be home by eleven," she shrieked. *Home by eleven?* Never once had she mentioned a curfew or asked where I'd been or where I was going. When I gave her some smart-ass rejoinder, she raised her hand to hit me. I lost it. "How dare you suddenly try to be a mother!" I yelled at her. "Everything's about you! So don't pretend for a minute you care about me and what time I come home." And instead of her slapping me, I slapped her. It felt good. She never raised a hand toward me again.

THE WORST COLLATERAL damage from all these moves was my education. When I went back to Fairfax to sign up for tenth-grade courses after our short stint in Brentwood, there were none available, at least not to me. I needed to make up credits, the school explained, and those courses were all filled. Why no one had told me about my lack of credits before I have no idea. Maybe they didn't care, or maybe I didn't.

The choices Fairfax presented to me were either to take noncredit courses like driver's ed or to switch to a special "continuation" school that was attached to Fairfax and attended by kids who were misfits or had drug issues or learning disabilities. I didn't fit into any of those categories, but that was the school I opted to attend, and I surprised myself by actively liking it and doing quite well there.

One thing was clear: I had to figure out a way to support myself so I could start leading my own life and escape from the crazy unpredictability of my mother's. And that's exactly what the continuation school offered: I entered a program called "four and four," which entailed four hours of classes and four hours of paid work, for which you earned credit. My very first job, which I got through a girlfriend at school, was with a collection agency. My slightly husky voice made me sound older than my age, and every afternoon I called and threatened people to pay up, or else. I kept waiting for my mom and dad to appear on the call lists.

It felt good to have my own pocket money and not have to rely on my mother, and it enabled me to enroll in an acting class—which turned out to be my salvation.

CHAPTER 5

Despite her financial straits, from time to time my mom and her friends would hit L.A. hot spots like Le Dome, where Jackie Collins always went for lunch with her friends. We were there one night when a man who looked to be in his late forties or early fifties came over to our table and introduced himself as Val Dumas. He said if we liked Le Dome, we should come by his restaurant, Mirabelle, sometime. He had a vaguely Middle Eastern appearance; I remember thinking he resembled Bijan, that quintessentially eighties icon who was always splashed across billboards in a tuxedo flogging his perfume. Val was a tall, elegant man with an air of superiority or money—or both—dressed in a soft button-down shirt and neatly pressed slacks, and Italian loafers. He chatted us up for a while, and then when my mom couldn't find her car keys, he offered us a ride home in his brown Mercedes but insisted I sit next to him in the passenger seat.

I had lunch with him at Mirabelle not long afterward. There were lots of plants, it had a relaxed, California-casual vibe, and the whole thing felt fun and harmless: it was broad daylight, and we were in public. I didn't question why a middle-aged man would want to hang out with a fifteen-year-old girl.

He started showing up at school, waiting for me outside in his car after classes let out. It was easier not having to take the bus, and often we'd stop at Mirabelle and have something to eat at his regular table. I told myself he was like a friend of the family, but there was something about him that made me slightly uneasy—an unsettling sense I had that he wouldn't always be so helpful and pleasant, a vague anxiety that there was something not quite right. I began to make excuses to avoid him.

Then one day when I got home from school he was there—inside the apartment, waiting for me. I felt the blood drain from my body. "What are you doing here?" I asked him. "Where's my mom?"

I have blotted out the exact sequence of events—the details that led from me opening the front door, to wondering if my mother had given him a key, to feeling trapped in my own home with a man three times my age and twice my size, to him raping me.

For decades, I didn't even think of it as rape. I thought of it as something I caused, something I felt obligated to do because this man expected it from me—I had let him expect it from me. I had eaten at his restaurant, and he had chauffeured me home from school. In my fifteen-year-old mind, I deserved what happened.

I couldn't see that—as someone with no guidance or grounding, no sense of worth, someone who'd spent her whole life contorting herself to meet other people's expectations—I was an easy mark for a predator.

And I had nobody to protect me.

In recent years, I have watched in awe as woman after woman has come forward to tell her story of sexual assault— amazed both by the courage of these women and by the attacks on their character that have inevitably followed. And yet people ask why it takes women years or decades to tell others what happened to them. All I can say is that anyone asking that question has never been raped. When you are sexually assaulted in a culture that tells you over and over again that admitting your victimization makes *you* a suspect—makes *you* a liar and a slut who deserves to have your life put under a microscope for all to see—guess what? You keep it a secret. And as with *any* trauma, denial is a natural human response. Things we can't handle, things that are just too frightening and destabilizing, the psyche suppresses until the day comes when we *can* deal with them.

Unfortunately, even as we try to submerge our pain deep down inside, it finds a way to bubble up: Through addiction. Through anxiety. Through eating disorders. Through insomnia. Through all the different PTSD symptoms and self-destructive behaviors that assault survivors experience for years on end.

These incidents may last minutes or hours, but their impact lasts a lifetime.

LESS THAN A week later, my mother told me we were moving again. I was happy to be getting out of the space where this ugly thing had happened to me—maybe if I was no longer surrounded by the walls of the apartment, I would stop feeling so disgusting, stop flashing back to staring at those walls while he was on top of me. But to my horror, Val showed up to help us move. I sat in the back seat of the Mercedes of the man who raped me, my mother sat with him up front, and he drove us to the cluster of Mediterranean-style duplexes off La Cienega where we were moving. Now there was nowhere safe to go: he'd be able to find me.

I felt like I was going to throw up as I got out of the car. Ginny was faster, plowing inside with her boxes, and in the seconds we were alone, Val turned to me and said, "How does it feel to be whored by your mother for five hundred dollars?" I stared at him blankly. And he said it again: "How does it feel to be whored by your mother for five hundred dollars?"

I'll never know if Ginny accepted five hundred dollars from Val explicitly as payment for permission to fuck me. Perhaps it was murkier than that—perhaps he gave her some money under the pretense of helping out a friend, as a loan on the deposit for the new apartment. For all I know she'd already paid him back by having sex with him herself. But what is certain is that she gave this man the key to the apartment she shared with her fifteen-year-old daughter. I've mothered three fifteen-year-old girls: the idea of giving a grown man with dubious intentions unsupervised access to them is as inconceivable to me as it is repugnant. That's not what a mother does.

And what I knew that day—what I know to *this* day—is that though Val may have given Ginny money with no clear discussion of what he would get in return, it's also entirely possible Ginny knew exactly what he wanted, and it's possible she agreed he could have it.

"How does it feel to be whored by your mother for five hundred dollars?" It feels like you are an orphan.

SOON AFTER WE moved to La Cienega I met a musician in my acting class, a pedal steel guitar player named Tom Dunston who'd been touring with Billy Joel. He was an attractive twenty-eight-year-old, with a gentle presence. He immediately made me feel at ease. We started hanging out, and one night when we were alone I started to take off my clothes. Tom stopped me. "You don't have to do that," he said. "We can just be together."

I told him about my mother's suicide attempts, and her using me as bait. I didn't talk about what had happened with Val. I never talked with anyone about what had happened with Val. By the time I met Tom, I had already walled it off behind the thickest plaster my psyche could construct. But I told him about everything else, and he listened.

So, when Tom invited me to move in with him, I said yes. He was waiting for me in his car when I walked out of my mother's apartment the day after my sixteenth birthday. I never went back.

CHAPTER 6

Years ago, I sat in on one of my daughter's sex-ed classes. The girls were told to be careful. They were warned about getting pregnant, and getting herpes, and all the other dangers of unprotected sex. But nobody said anything about pleasure. Nobody told them about the gift of intimacy and sensuousness that sex can offer. There was nothing to help them understand how their bodies even worked, let alone how to love them.

Which seems like such a mistake. I feel that if I'd had some of that—some information, some education, some sense of what would constitute healthy and desirable sex—I would have been better equipped to protect myself from sex that was exploitative. I would have recognized unhealthy or abusive encounters, because I would have had some idea of a version of sex that was *mutual* and *pleasurable*. I might not have been so quick to assume that anytime something happened that made me feel terrible, it was my fault and meant there was something wrong with me. I might not have felt that if a man demanded sex from me, it was my obligation to give it to him because I'd put myself in a position that made him think he was entitled to use my body.

Granted, I didn't exactly have the kind of parental support that would lead me to value myself on that level. But I wish I'd been taught—by someone, somewhere—about my body, what was possible in a sexual relationship, how to consider my own desires instead of seeing sex as degrading or something I owed someone. Or as a way to get male validation of my worth.

THOUGH TOM DUNSTON was twenty-eight and I was only sixteen when I moved in with him, we had a surprisingly healthy dynamic. He never treated me with anything but care and respect. His mom, an executive assistant to one of Aaron Spelling's top producers—*Vegas* was his big show at the time—got me a job as her receptionist at Twentieth Century Fox, even though she disapproved of my living with her son, what with our age difference. (It wasn't just out of the goodness of her heart. I always thought she did it to make sure I could pay my half of the living expenses.) But Tom and I had a stable, comfortable routine: he dropped me off at the continuation school at Fairfax High every morning, then I went to my job, and he picked me up in the evenings on the way to our acting class. He also got me into the L.A. music scene, which was exploding at that time: we hit the Troubadour, Starwood, the Whisky a Go Go, Madame Wong's, seeing at least two bands a week—The Go-Go's, The Knack, The Motels, Billy Idol, The Police. It was very much about the music and the excitement of the scene: I didn't drink, partly because I was underage and partly because I saw it as a way of separating myself from my mother.

For maybe six months, I had barely any contact with Ginny. I was angry at her for being a train wreck; she was angry at me for "abandoning" her. My dad was almost entirely absent from my life, too: he had moved back to Roswell with Morgan to live with my uncle Buddy. But Tom and I were like our own little family.

Still, against all odds, I felt drawn to my parents. When my mother begged me to go with her to visit my aunt in Albuquerque, I was unable to resist.

"Don't go," Tom said. "You can't trust her. It isn't going to be any different than it was before." He tried his best to tell me—to protect me. But it had been months since I'd seen my mother.

Tom was right, of course. Only hours after we'd arrived in Albuquerque, my mother started a screaming fight with my aunt—I can't remember what set her off, but I can tell you for sure it was unimportant, some perceived slight that could have been easily resolved with a calm conversation. "We're out of here!" she shrieked, and told me we were going to my grandmother's in Roswell. I was disgusted with her and angry at my-self. The trip had been a mistake. I just wanted to get back to L.A. and my calm life with Tom.

Ginny wouldn't give me my plane ticket. She was furious that I wouldn't do what she wanted—she accused me of being a ter-rible daughter, of thinking I was too good for her, of taking her for granted. She slammed the door behind her and plowed out of my aunt's driveway in a rage. So there I was, stranded in New Mexico, without the money to get back home. I had to ask my aunt if I could borrow the seventy-five dollars for a new plane ticket. The guilt I felt—for years—for owing her that money would be difficult to overstate. It seemed like something my parents would do: show up at someone's house and then, in-stead of thanking them for their hospitality, ask them for money. It was the opposite of who I wanted to be.

The next day at the airport waiting to fly home, I thought about what a complete mess my parents were and felt very deeply alone. Your mother and father are supposed to act as a kind of touchstone along the path to the future—offering in-sight on what to reach for, what to look forward to. For me, that picture was dismal.

I went out onto the tarmac to board, and as I was walking toward the plane with the other passengers, I heard my name. I turned and saw a police officer in uniform approaching me. "Are you Demi Guynes?" he asked. I nodded, confused, and he said, "You need to come with me." He took me by the arm and led me away while the other passengers gawked like I was a criminal. "Your parents are here," he told me, as he walked me into a little room where, sure enough, Ginny *and* Danny were waiting for me.

I stammered, "What the hell is going on?"

My mother gave a triumphant little smile. "You're under eighteen," she replied with satisfaction. "We reported you to the police as a runaway." I could tell from her speech that she'd been drinking. My father was so wasted his eyes were completely glassy. I turned to the cop who had brought me in. "Can't you see they're drunk?" I asked, furious, adrenaline pumping through my body. I don't know that I've ever been angrier: the complete injustice of the situation was just too much. And the dishonesty! Like they cared about my well-being? As if they were these concerned, normal parents? "You're making a huge mistake! You don't know what you're doing," I told the policeman. "I haven't lived with either of them in over six months!" I could tell he was starting to recognize that something was wrong with this picture. Ginny and Danny had probably been sitting there getting more and more inebriated while he'd been out looking for me. Of the three of us, I was clearly the closest thing to an adult. "I'm so sorry," the cop said quietly. But I *was* under eighteen, and he didn't have much choice.

So I was stuck with them. These two lying, alcoholic, divorced people—who last I'd heard weren't speaking—were my parents; they had ensnared me, and they demanded I return to Roswell with them. The hours while we waited for that plane—and they continued drinking at the airport bar—felt endless.

After we landed, we got in the car they'd left at the airport in Roswell, but my dad was so wasted he got pulled over by the police on the drive back. Unbelievably, he managed to sweet-talk his way out of a ticket. (My brother always says my dad could sell ice cubes to Eskimos, and that incident was proof.) It was the middle of the night when we reached the house my dad was sharing with my uncle Buddy, who, it became clear, was every bit as drunk as my father—Buddy was just getting home after the bars closed. Morgan wasn't there, and I couldn't even look at my mother, who was barely paying attention to me at this point anyway: she had only been interested in winning a power struggle, and once she was victorious, she went back to focusing on herself. Before long, Buddy and my dad were fighting, lurching drunkenly through the house, everything becoming violent and out of control. When I saw my dad pull out his gun and start waving it at Buddy, I thought, *That's enough.* It was very late, and the sky was black and moonless, but the world outside that house was less frightening than the one inside it. I walked out the door and kept going for four miles along the unlit roads until I reached my grandma Marie's house.

It was one thirty in the morning. I was so sorry for my grandmother: that I was waking her up in the middle of the night; that my parents had obviously weaseled money out of her for their plane tickets to go and "save" me at the airport in Albuquerque; that she had to put up with these people and their insanity altogether. I was apologizing and telling her what had happened, and she wanted me to call Ginny and tell her where

I was so my parents wouldn't worry. "They don't care about me," I said, and at that moment, I knew I was telling the truth.

Forty years later, I no longer think of it in those terms. They loved me. But they loved me the way they loved each other, the only way they knew how: inconsistently and conditionally. From them, I learned that love was something you had to scramble to keep. It could be revoked at any minute, for reasons that you couldn't understand, that you couldn't control. The kind of love I grew up with was scary to need, and painful to feel. If I didn't have that uneasy ache, that prickly anxiety around someone, how would I know it was love?

CHAPTER 7

Tom took me to see a new band called The Kats; they were a big deal at the time. The star was a guitarist from Minneapolis named Freddy Moore, and he changed my life—or at least my name.

Freddy wrote most of the band's songs, and played guitar and sang. He was absolutely electric onstage, with his shaggy blond hair, sharp features, and wild blue eyes—a totally magnetic performer. I went back to the Troubadour to see the band again on my own. Watching Freddy, I was blown away: if I could be with someone that captivating, then maybe I would be captivating, too. Between sets I maneuvered Freddy into the bathroom. Within a month, I'd left Tom to move in with him.

Our instant attraction reflected the spontaneity and free-spiritedness you feel when you're young and your whole life is stretched out in front of you, and you don't focus on the consequences of your actions. Unfortunately, when I broke up with Tom, I didn't treat him with anywhere near the consideration he'd shown me, and I glossed over the fact that Freddy was twenty-nine and still married to his high school sweetheart from Minnesota. When he left her for me, I was only sixteen. I was a self-absorbed teenager who hadn't been raised with a lot of respect for the institution of marriage, and I jumped into life with Freddy without, I'm sorry to say, much concern for his wife. Then again, he was almost twice my age, and he was the one who was married. But age is confusing: throughout my life I've been in relationships where power and maturity don't necessarily lie with whoever is older.

Offstage, Freddy was a different person: quiet and focused and very disciplined, carving out time every day to sit down and write his music. He encouraged me to be creative, too—I wrote a song with him called "Changing," which he ended up recording with Mark Linett, the engineer who had worked on all of Brian Wilson's music. The Kats had a small-time manager when Freddy and I first got together, and they used to tour in this really old Chevy Suburban that pulled a trailer with all their equipment in it. I'd go along, either in the Suburban with the musicians and their wives or girlfriends, or I'd drive in the beat-up old Volkswagen I'd bought, with lawn chairs for a back seat, a hole in the floorboard, and a bad paint job. We slept late and went to gigs every night.

I quit school. Obviously, when I left Tom, I'd lost my job working for his mom. Freddy's manager had warned him that I might just be after his money—which is pretty funny, considering they didn't make any—so I was eager to prove that I could pay my own way. When a friend I'd met through the music scene told me about a guy she knew who took nude photos and sold them to magazines in Japan, I was curious. "Nobody sees them here, and you can make some money," she told me. "Just lie about your age." I went for it.

The shoot took place in a dark, old industrial building in West Hollywood. I was uncomfortable, worried that I would be confronted with a bad situation, but I had committed to doing it. I found my way to a cheesy faux living room, with couches, chairs, and throw pillows. Fortunately, the photographer turned out to be very professional, even as he was encouraging me to strike all sorts of provocative poses. I was comforted when he told me about a Japanese law prohibiting photos showing pubic hair—I could tell myself I was only posing *semi*nude, which seemed much better than the alternative. The session went well, but I felt weird about it. I never did those Japanese nudes again.

They were my ticket into more modeling, though. Soon after my photos began circulating around Japan, I got another offer to do some pictures for *Oui* magazine. *Playboy* had originally imported *Oui* from France to attract a younger readership. It was a legitimate magazine, and I had to sign a proper release that specified that because I was underage, I could be on the cover and show cleavage, but I couldn't pose nude for the inside of the magazine—which was a total relief from my point of view.

I was very lucky that I happened to get paired with the well-known fashion photographer Philip Dixon for the shoot. Philip asked me to work with him again, modeling for a swimsuit catalog he was shooting. I was anxious because I didn't think I had a great body—no waist, still carrying some baby fat—but Philip made me look beautiful. I started to think maybe I could make a living as a model instead of having to get a regular job to pay the bills while I was pursuing acting.

I took Philip's pictures and some headshots to Elite Model Management, and they signed me. I was thrilled, even though at first I didn't get any major assignments, just little local jobs like newspaper ads for department stores and the poster for the cult horror movie *I Spit on Your Grave*. I earned just enough to squeak by.

It's funny: modeling was the first thing in my life that gave me a tiny taste of success, that stirred a sense of pride and professionalism in me, which was empowering. But at the same time, it threw me into a world that seemed tailor-made to lower my self-esteem. I had landed in a profession that focused entirely on how I looked, and what size I wore, which reinforced the idea I'd absorbed that my value lay solely in my attractiveness.

I dropped out of acting class. It was awkward seeing Tom there, and I think on some level I was terrified that they'd tell me, "You're not good enough; you can't be an actor." For most people, auditioning is the scary part. For me, not measuring up in class was more terrifying. The way I was raised, always bailing before I had to follow through, was also a factor—I had no experience with perseverance. Today I would without question tell someone trying to make it as an actor, "Go put yourself in class! Go learn, go boost your confidence, get to know the tools you can use, get to know *yourself.*"

MY DAD WAS now living with Morgan, who'd turned twelve, in Oceanside, California. Freddy and I went to see them for Christmas. Pulling up to the building where they were living in a small, depressing, nondescript apartment, my heart sank. My father looked terrible, as bad as the setting. There are some people you can look at and not really see their pain. On my dad it was unmistakable—in his bloated face, his slumped posture, and his vacant eyes.

I remember sitting at the kitchen table on Christmas Day feeling the emptiness of us spending the holiday with just my dad and my little brother, split off from the rest of the family. Freddy—who, I realize now, was only a few years younger than my dad—was socially awkward in general, and this setting was no exception. He was a classic quiet Minnesotan with Scandinavian roots: taciturn, pragmatic, recessive. It's not like he didn't care about me, he was just inexpressive. I was the only one at that table scrambling to connect.

As a present, my dad gave me a random poster—something completely impersonal that had nothing to do with me or, for that matter, him. He was drinking heavily and so was fairly out of it, and I worried about what kind of care my dad, in his defeated state, could be providing for Morgan. I chatted nervously about the different things I had going on, self-consciously aware that it was uncomfortable for my dad to look at me, that he didn't know what to say.

The most painful thing for me had not been finding out that Danny wasn't my biological father, but finding that he was incapable of reaching out to reassure me that he loved me regardless. Now, I wish that *I* had reached out to *him*—grabbed him, looked him in the eyes, told him that he was my dad from the start and would be my dad till the end, and that I loved him.

Not long after I returned to Los Angeles, I got a call that Danny was in the hospital. His liver had ruptured. He tried to drive himself to the emergency room but didn't quite make it; they found him passed out in the car—leaning on the horn, fortunately—at the entrance to the hospital, and rushed him inside. He recovered from that episode, but a doctor informed him that he was an alcoholic with pancreatitis and needed to stop drinking immediately. My dad was so furious at that doctor he threatened to use everything in his power to ruin him if the doctor put that in his medical record. He must have been pretty intimidating, because the doctor rescinded his diagnosis. The doctor also said he couldn't eat red meat anymore, so Dad immediately opened an account at the local butcher shop, Morgan later told me, and he started eating triple the amount of red meat he had before. Everything he was told not to do, he did it in spades. He was slowly trying to kill himself. He told me many times that he wanted to die. When I think of what it must have been like for Morgan as a twelve-year-old hearing from his own father how much he wanted his life to end, it breaks my heart.

Back in New Mexico a year later, it was Morgan who found Dad in his garage, slumped over the steering wheel of his car with the engine running, after he committed suicide. He was thirty-six.

When I got the call, I burst into tears. I was sitting at the dining room table with Freddy. He didn't come over to hold me or comfort me. He didn't tell me that he loved me and that everything would be okay. He sat still in his seat and said calmly, "There's no point in crying; there's nothing you can do now. It's not going to change anything."

THE FUNERAL IN Roswell was a nightmare. Instead of shared grief, there were warring camps—my dad's family and my mom. My parents had spent the weekend before Dad died together, and my dad's eight siblings were convinced that Ginny was somehow to blame for his death. There were various theories, ranging from speculation that she had driven him to it, to the idea that she'd left him drunk in his car knowing what would happen, all the way up to the suspicion of out-and-out foul play, with my dad's family threatening to turn Ginny in to the police. It got very, very ugly. DeAnna remembers that even her husband, my uncle George, was convinced that Ginny was responsible.

The truth is that my dad had probably planned his own death to the last detail. His blood alcohol level was so high that his death had to be ruled an accident—he was too drunk for the insurance company to label it a suicide. Consequently, they were obliged to make a small payout, which Dad left to Morgan. I guarantee you my dad had done his research and knew precisely how much he had to drink for all of that to happen. It was his final scam, one for the road. But it was also, obviously, a way of ending the pain he was carrying, which had become too much to bear. He felt he had failed us all, and I think that, on some level, he really believed he was doing the best thing for everyone.

Meanwhile, over at my grandmother's house, my mother's sisters half-heartedly rallied around Ginny, trying to show some solidarity. But my mom was in full-blown victim mode, crying uncontrollably and inserting herself into the center of the unfolding drama. She tried to insist that Danny be dressed in the suit she picked out for the wake, but my dad's sister Margie wanted him in the brown suit she'd selected. It escalated from there: Margie went over to my dad's house and took everything of value and hid it from Ginny. The funeral home was providing cars for the family, and my mother demanded to be in one. His siblings were furious that she'd even ask: She wasn't his wife anymore, what was she even doing there? And so on. It felt like my dad's family's anger at my mother was spilling over onto me, as if I was an extension of Ginny. (In fact, the only substantial interaction I remember having with her the whole time I was there was a fight about what I was going to wear.) Everybody knew that Danny wasn't my biological father, and suddenly it felt like that mattered enormously. *Do I even belong in this family?* Maybe I was being hypersensitive, but I felt unwelcome and uncomfortable. *Is it okay that I'm here?* Not *here* here, at this funeral, but here on this earth. *Is it okay that I was even born?*

MY DAD DIED in October. I turned eighteen in November. I got married to Freddy the following February. It was obviously a confusing and fraught time, and our wedding reflected the scattershot nature of the decision. DeAnna and George were the only members of my family who came. I wore a vintage dress, with flowers tucked behind my veil. It was at some little Spanish church in L.A. I can't remember where.

PART II
SUCCESS

CHAPTER 8

As my family was disintegrating, my career was picking up. A bunch of breaks came my way in rapid succession. First, John Casablancas, the legendary owner of Elite, picked me to go with a handful of other girls to New York City. It was incredibly exciting. They flew me there and put me up, paid for new headshots geared toward New York's high fashion market, and sent me on "go-sees": interviews with potential clients. The city was overwhelming—and intimidating. And it smelled! I still remember the first time I saw steam billowing up from a manhole in Manhattan—it was like there was an underworld of fire just below the city's surface, burning night and day.

Freddy came with me, and I had mixed feelings about that. On the one hand, I would have been anxious about going to Manhattan for the first time by myself, but on the other, I worried his band couldn't keep going without him, and sure enough, once he told the rest of The Kats of his plan to spend some time in New York, they all got other gigs. I was nervous that Freddy was putting all his eggs in my basket. I, meanwhile, was beyond driven—hell-bent on getting out of the dysfunctional place I'd come from and into the bright world of success, where I imagined people lived happy, normal lives. (Ha.) Freddy and I were going in different directions, and I began to pull away from him.

I was in New York for several months. I got cast in a commercial, and Freddy and I moved into a tiny little apartment on the Upper West Side. On the last day of shooting, I felt that familiar tightness in my body that signaled a kidney flare-up, but I told myself it was just the hot lights.

We were scheduled to return to Los Angeles the next day. By the time we landed, I had blown up like a balloon; I was swollen from head to toe. Freddy had no idea what to do, but fortunately I had called DeAnna, who was waiting for us at the airport and took me straight to the emergency room at UCLA. I was retaining so much fluid at that point, I still have stretch marks up and down my legs.

This attack was different. By now, a lot more was known about the disease—they didn't have to keep me at the hospital for months; once I was stabilized they sent me home on a high dose of Prednisone.

There was another difference. In the past, my flare-ups had always followed one of my dad's infidelities. This time, the infidelity was mine. I had tried to repress it, but my body wouldn't let me.

The night before we got married, instead of working on my vows, I was calling a guy I'd met on a movie set. I snuck out of my own bachelorette party and went to his apartment.

Why did I do that? Why didn't I go and see the man I was committing to spend the rest of my life with to express my doubts? Because I couldn't face the fact that I was getting married to distract myself from grieving the death of my father. Because I felt there was no room to question what I'd already put in motion. I couldn't get out of the marriage, but I could sabotage it.

Only it's not much of a sabotage when it's a secret. You just end up sabotaging yourself.

A FEW MONTHS later, I got my second big break: an audition for *General Hospital*. I'd never watched a soap opera, but I knew this was a huge deal. For one thing, it was the number one show on daytime television. For another, *GH* was in the press a lot right then, because the actress Genie Francis, who played Laura Spencer—of the famous Luke and Laura—was retiring, and no less a celebrity than Elizabeth Taylor was doing a kind of extended cameo on the show. I was extremely nervous when I went in to read for this classic soap, which had been on the air for two decades. But I tried to picture myself back by the swimming pool on Kings Road, reading scripts to Nastassja. That helped get me through it. Also, I loved the part: Jackie Templeton, a sharp, no-nonsense, plucky young reporter. They wanted a "Margot Kidder type," someone like the actress who played Lois Lane in *Superman*, which had been wildly popular in theaters a few years earlier. I had Kidder's dark hair and green eyes, and we had something else in common: a husky voice. There's something about that slight rasp that people find compelling—I guess because it suggests toughness and vulnerability at the same time. I got the part.

It was intoxicating and terrifying. Jackie Templeton turned out to be a really big role. And in general, soaps are just hard work—different from other television, and definitely different from film; there is no other medium where an actor is given thirty pages to memorize and film in a day. We'd get a script maybe a couple of days in advance, but there was a limit to how much dialogue one could really manage beyond the day ahead. On the weekend you might get a couple scripts at once so you could see where the story was going, but the daily thrust was always: here are your scenes; deal with them!

The rewards of this scramble were huge. For the first time in my life, *I* was in control of whether I could make rent, eat, afford new clothes, pay the utility bill. When I started the show, I was so embarrassed by my beat-up Volkswagen that I wouldn't drive onto the studio lot; I'd park it on the street and then walk in the gate. I remember feeling mortified one day when one of the guards said, "You know you can park on the lot, right?," and I realized he'd seen me in the car. The first thing I bought when I saved up enough money was a brand-new silver Honda Accord. I was so proud as I drove it past the guards and into my reserved parking spot.

In many ways *General Hospital* was like another new school I had to figure out, but the stakes were much higher. While I saw soaps as a stepping-stone, I realized the show had the power to change my life for the better, and I didn't want people to see my weaknesses or sense my insecurity. On the surface I was hitting all my marks, but my internal compass sought outlets for my self-doubt. I started drinking.

There was often free time during the day when someone else's character was being taped, but not enough time to leave the building and go anywhere, so I hung out with Tony Geary, who played Luke, in his dressing room when we weren't needed on the set. Tony always had some kind of liquor on hand, which he disguised by mixing it with Coke. I never turned down his offer of a drink. He was the star of the show, after all, and if that's how the star behaved, then it must be okay.

Freddy and I didn't have more than the occasional beer at home. The problem was, when I did have a drink, I couldn't stop; there was no little voice in my head saying, *That's enough, Demi*. There were no brakes. One night, Freddy and I went to hear an up-and-coming New Wave band. As they moved through their set, I had one drink, then another, then another. Backstage, after the gig, I was talking to somebody from the band when I blacked out. The next thing I remember is him yelling at me in a heavy English accent. I have no idea what I said to him, but it must have been pretty bad. "Get out!" he screamed. "Get the fuck out!" That sobered me up quickly. Heads turned to look as Freddy rushed me to the door. That was my first major booze-related humiliation.

It's one thing to get wasted at a club late at night. It's another to get drunk while you're working.

I was invited with several of the stars of *General Hospital* to fly somewhere to do a live panel for a dedicated soap audience. My unraveling began on the plane when I started ordering drinks from the stewardess, and accelerated when I got to the hotel and cleared out the minibar. I was so intoxicated by the time the panel began that I couldn't stay upright in my seat.

The next day, I was horrified. It felt too out of control, too much like my parents. I knew that alcohol was moving me in their direction, back to where I came from, instead of forward into the future I envisioned for myself. I quit drinking, cold turkey.

BREAK NUMBER THREE came just after I turned twenty, in 1982, when I auditioned for a part in my first real movie and got it. My dream had always been movies, and everything about this one, *Blame It on Rio*, was intoxicating. It was shooting in a foreign country, and so for the first time in my life, I got a passport. It was with a big studio, directed by the legendary Stanley Donen, who'd made classics like *Singin' in the Rain*, *Damn Yankees!*, and *Charade*. Valerie Harper was playing my mother—I'd grown up watching her on *The Mary Tyler Moore Show* and *Rhoda*. And Michael Caine was playing my father. I didn't truly understand what that meant at the time, what a unique opportunity this was to work with one of the world's great actors, I just knew that I was excited to be in a movie. I negotiated three months off from my *General Hospital* contract to do the film.

I went to Brazil feeling—as I had many times in my life— like this was a new start: a whole new ball game. It was a pattern I'd gotten used to. If something wasn't working, I knew in a short while we'd be gone, so I didn't have to try to fix whatever it was. And if it was working? Well, enjoy it, because it'll be over before you know it.

We were staying in a big hotel on Ipanema Beach, and the first night we all met for dinner. There was Michael Caine and his wife, Shakira, who was so elegant, exotic, and sophisticated— really something to behold for a grubby kid from New Mexico. Joe Bologna, the other male lead, was a total mensch, extremely warm; in truth, everyone went out of their way to make me feel comfortable. I was in awe, soaking it all up but trying to act cool. I wanted them to see whatever they wanted to see. I told myself, *Don't fuck this up. Sit still, watch, and learn.*

The film itself was really a dirty old man's fantasy—it could never be made today—but at that time, it seemed perfectly normal. I played a seventeen-year-old on vacation in Rio with my best friend, who basically seduces my father against his will. Joe Bologna played the friend's father, and I was the supporting actress. The lead, Michelle Johnson, was a young model who'd been plucked out of obscurity in Phoenix, Arizona, and I think her breasts were a major factor in the casting—which also seemed par for the course in those days. She struck me as quite innocent. Even though I was not much older than she was, I felt like a veteran by comparison.

On set, I met a very cool local girl named Zezé, who had signed up to be an extra in the movie just for fun. Zezé came from a wealthy family; she was well educated and spoke perfect English. We became friends and quickly got a great little groove going. In our free time, she showed me around Rio, took me to restaurants, and introduced me to her friends. We all started going to lots of parties together, and it was a blast.

Freddy wasn't there, and I was just me in a place where I had no history, so I could experiment with figuring out the *me* I wanted to be, without any encumbrances. It was an awakening in so many expansive and positive ways, offset, unfortunately, by a *lot* of cocaine. I nearly burned a hole through my nostrils while I was in Brazil.

The studio was putting me up in a very nice hotel and giving me a per diem allowance as well, so the living was easy. It became even easier when Zezé pointed out that I could rent a furnished apartment, and she helped me find a great one, overlooking the beach. We'd befriended Peter, a young guy who was running the second unit camera on the movie, and he became my roommate. Peter and I split the rent, and I pocketed the extra money from my allowance and put it toward cocaine. My Brazilian friends would get it for me, and they got very good stuff. Everybody in Rio seemed to be doing coke—and drinking, except, ironically, for me. I didn't drink because I knew, *I can't handle that. It's not safe for me.* I didn't give a second thought to the effects of cocaine. In my mind, I'd found this thing that made me feel up and productive and creative, so what could be wrong with it? I had the cash to keep myself well supplied, and because I had a relatively small part in the movie, I had a fair amount of time off to enjoy it.

It was a delicious few months. I had made a lifelong friend in Zezé—we're still close to this day. We hung out with Peter and Zezé's friend Paolo, a beautiful Brazilian boy, all the time, partying at our apartment, going to the beach, and exploring the city. It was easy to forget I was married—to the point that one night Peter and I ended up in bed. (We both recognized it was a mistake right away; it only happened that once.) I was having an adventure. I was gaining momentum in my career. And I had never felt so free.

All that freedom—combined with my youth, not to mention the extra boost of bravado and heedlessness that cocaine gives you—led me to push the envelope. My character was supposed to hang glide in the movie, but because of an insurance issue the producers were insisting on a stunt double. But Peter was the second unit director, and I told him, "Come on, just let me do it."

It could have cost him his job; it could have put the movie at risk. It was an idea borne of drug-fueled recklessness, but it happened to work out. I slipped on the harness and ran right off the edge of a cliff over the Atlantic Ocean. The view was unbelievable.

CHAPTER 9

Even as I was acting out in Brazil, I was having a kind of epiphany about honesty. The person I wanted to be didn't lie. When I got back from Rio, I was determined to be completely truthful with Freddy, to take responsibility for what I'd done and what I wanted. I came clean with my husband about what had happened with Peter and told him I thought our marriage wasn't working.

He was angry. And I understood. I had failed him in our marriage; I wanted to do the right thing in our divorce, so I agreed to pay him alimony for a year. He wasn't alone for long, though. Early in our relationship, he'd given guitar lessons to make extra money, and one of his students was a friend's fourteen-year-old sister. I noticed right away that Freddy and Renee had a connection—despite his being more than twice her age—and one afternoon I told them, "If anything ever happened to Freddy and me, I bet you two would get together." Renee was embarrassed, and he was furious with me for upsetting her at the time, but as soon as Freddy and I broke up, they got together, and they're still a couple to this day.

The divorce had been my idea, but I still felt adrift after we split. A friend lent me his apartment in Marina del Rey until I found a place of my own, and that's where I camped out. I turned twenty-one in that apartment, alone.

I wasn't really close with anyone from *General Hospital*, where I'd returned to work off the remainder of my contract after I got back from Brazil. I took a second leave from my job there to do another movie, but it fell through. By then, *General Hospital* had already written me out of the upcoming story line. Suddenly, I didn't have anything to distract me from myself.

I started drinking again. It was a really dark time for me. The self I presented to the world was the same it had always been—upbeat, confident, daring. I bought a Kawasaki motorcycle and sped around Los Angeles without a helmet. I didn't even have a license for the bike.

My appetite for cocaine had escalated into a dependency, and though I would never have called myself an addict, that's what I had become. I got some of my cocaine from a dentist, so it was really good stuff, and when that was unavailable, I got my coke through my business manager. It seems incredible to me now that the person advising me on my finances never once drew my attention to all the money I was spending on drugs, but then again, he was using them, too. I got out of that arrangement with him eventually, but not before I'd blown through most my money.

Fortunately, I landed a lead part in *No Small Affair*, a romantic teen comedy Columbia Pictures was distributing. I played a young nightclub singer, and Jon Cryer played the nineteen-year-old photographer who falls in love with her, in his first movie role. Jon fell for me in real life, too, and lost his virginity to me while we were making that movie. It pains me to think of how callous I was with his feelings—that I stole what could have been such an important and beautiful moment from him. I was sort of losing it right then, and I was definitely not in a place to take care of someone else's feelings. I started to do some seriously self-destructive things during that period—I remember waking up not knowing where I was, thinking, *Am I supposed to be at work in an hour?*, and then having to call someone and ask to be picked up. It's all a blur.

Craig Baumgarten, a studio executive at Columbia, took me under his wing while we were making *No Small Affair*. He was going away for a while, and he offered to let me stay in his house. I was very wary when he invited me to come see the place, but in a great step forward for me, I didn't sleep with him, and he didn't push me to. I think he was genuinely fond of me, but he was crazy to let me stay in his very grown-up house in Beverly Hills in my state, and even crazier to give me the keys to his wife's Jaguar. "Use the car," he said. "It's just sitting there." And so I did, excited to be cruising around Los Angeles in style. Somehow, I didn't wreck it, thank God.

I went hunting for my own place. Moving from house to house in rapid succession had felt familiar in the worst way, and I wanted a real home. I found the perfect tiny two-bedroom on Willoughby with a black-and-white linoleum floor in the kitchen. The front of the house was completely hidden by a fence covered with winding vines, so it was very private, and the inside was immaculate. I loved it there. I never got a couch for the living room, and the second bedroom had just a mattress on the floor, but the house gave me something to put my energy into, as well as a sense of independence and grounding. It was the first place I ever owned.

True to form, within weeks of my move, my mother showed up at my doorstep with her new young boyfriend and Morgan. She needed a place for them to stay while she looked for an apartment, she told me. She seemed worse than ever. They crashed in my tiny house for a few weeks; I knew if I let them stay any longer, I'd never get them out. I wouldn't have minded if it was just Morgan. (And neither would my girlfriends: he was sixteen and growing into his looks.) But he was a teenager now, no longer a fragile little boy. In fact, he was in military school back in Roswell; he had decided he needed some structure and sanity in his life—which I understood too well.

Time's up, I told Ginny: you've got to go.

I GOT A call from my agent, Hildy Gottlieb, saying Sony wanted me to audition for a new movie by John Hughes, who had made a big name for himself directing a series of hits about teen-agers: *Sixteen Candles*, *The Breakfast Club*, *Weird Science*. The morning of the audition, I got on my motorcycle and took off for the studio, where Hughes was holding a general cast-ing session. I did all right in the audition, but it seemed like Hughes wasn't impressed, and I didn't think I'd get a part.

I was walking down the hall after the audition when I heard footsteps hurrying after me. "Miss, miss," a voice was calling, but I didn't stop, assuming there had to be some other "miss" this guy was pursuing. I was halfway down the stairs when he caught up to me, panting.

"Are you an actress?" he asked.

"Who wants to know?" I said.

"Joel Schumacher," he replied, "my boss."

Joel would recount this story over and over again for years to come. *Vanity Fair* quoted him in a 1991 article as saying he'd seen "this flash running down the stairs—she had long black hair down to the waist, she was incredible-looking, like a young Arabian racehorse." So he sent his assistant after me and had me come in to read for the part of Jules, in his new film with Columbia Pictures, *St. Elmo's Fire*.

Jules was, fittingly, a party girl who was developing a cocaine habit. She was one of seven recent graduates of Georgetown University who were trying to find their way in the adult world and would meet regularly at a bar called St. Elmo's. It had that dynamic energy about it, like it was really going to be some-thing. And, in the wake of the John Hughes movies that were so popular, it felt like a whole new generation was coming into focus on-screen. *St. Elmo's Fire* would star Rob Lowe, Emilio Estevez, Ally Sheedy, Judd Nelson, Mare Winningham, Andrew McCarthy, and me.

Memory—especially memory clouded by drugs—is a funny thing. In his own memoir, Rob suggests that we had some kind of hot-and-heavy romance; I can vaguely recall one ill-advised late night together, but I'm grateful to him for the complimentary descriptions of our youth. In truth, I liked all my costars and remain close to some of them today, but the person who stands out from this period is, of course, Emilio.

I met Emilio the day we were each having our screen tests, and we started talking right away. He had a quiet confidence, which was very attractive to me—he seemed so grounded— and he had a great sense of humor, too. I loved his looks: his sand-colored hair and piercing blue eyes, the lovely structure of his face and his chiseled features. As rehearsals got under way, we began to hang out.

But Emilio was a very disciplined person; he consumed alcohol like a normal person, and he didn't smoke or take drugs. I kept that side of myself out of his sight. Zezé had moved to L.A. and was living with me now, and we did a lot of coke together. Actually, I did a lot more than she did: at my peak I was going through an eighth of an ounce every two days by myself.

I guess there were rumors about my partying, because one day when I was at the studio having a fitting in wardrobe, Joel Schumacher suddenly appeared in the room. "If I hear of you having even one beer, you're fired," he announced in a loud voice in front of all the others. Then he turned on his heel and walked out. I felt like I had been punched. For him to dress me down in front of other people was demeaning and released such an immediate flood of shame that I felt physically sick.

Soon after that incident, I got a call from Craig Baumgarten, who had lent me his house and was still kind of keeping an eye on me, at least partly because he had vested professional interest in *St. Elmo's* working out. "This is what you're going to do," he instructed me mysteriously but firmly. "There's a place in Redondo Beach, and unless you're dead or dying, you're going to show up there tomorrow. They're expecting you." I wasn't sure exactly what this place was, but he gave me the address. I knew he was serious when the assistant I'd just hired told me I had an appointment scheduled for the next morning and that she was going to take me there herself; he'd called her, too.

I had already planned dinner that night with my friend Tim Van Patten, whom I'd met shooting the pilot for a TV show that never went anywhere, and a friend of his at a sushi restaurant on Melrose. At first I was careful with my drinking—no hard alcohol, that was my rule—but as I watched Timmy and his friend doing shots, I thought, *What the hell.*

One drink led to another, and then another at the next bar. I was joking with Tim about the effects of alcohol versus cocaine when I laughingly heard myself say, "I'm a drug addict," as if it were a big joke. But it didn't feel like a joke. I had never said those words before or admitted that to myself and suddenly I stopped laughing and started to cry. "No, I really am," I told him. It was the truth.

He must have gotten me home because I ended up on the bathroom floor, where Zezé found me drunk and writhing like a crazy person. "There's a demon inside me, and I have to get it out!" I told her. Zezé managed to talk me down and get me safely into bed, but she must have been terrified.

When I woke up the next morning, I remembered the appointment. Without even thinking, I went straight to look for whatever cocaine was left, and that's what I had for breakfast. My assistant picked me up and took me to the address in Redondo Beach, which turned out to be a hospital. I clearly remember going up in the elevator and walking down a long corridor toward a sign that read: ALCOHOL REHABILITATION CENTER.

My gut reaction was, "No. That's for my mom. *I'm* a drug addict." But I'd been ordered to report to rehab unless I was dying, and though I might have wanted to be at that moment, what I wanted even more was to protect my career.

REHAB WAS STILL very fringe in 1984. The Betty Ford clinic, in many ways the prototype for the industry, had opened only two years before. Many of the people in my rehab in Redondo Beach had been drinking their whole lives and had decades of horror stories to share. I didn't have that long a track record: I was only twenty-one, and had been wrestling with alcohol issues off and on for three years, and with cocaine for maybe two. That didn't mean my dependency was minor, though. When the head of admission told me their program lasted *thirty* days I was aghast. Thirty days! That was just impossible.

"We're starting to shoot a movie in sixteen days," I said.

She asked me, "What's more important? The film or your life?"

"The film!" I told her, and I meant it.

"There is no film if you have no life," she pointed out. "I'd like to put you in a bed right now." I felt like I might jump out of my skin. I told her I had to go to the bathroom. Inside the stall, I rummaged through my pockets for a used vial of coke to scavenge one last hit. Then I went back to the counselor's office and told her, "I cannot *not* do this film. It's all that I've got."

I don't know if there was something in the way I said it, but she studied my face for a minute and then said, "Let me make a call. But at least stay tonight."

The clinic staff clearly assumed I was going to be admitted for the duration because there was already a bag waiting for me, filled with all the stuff I could possibly need to move in for a month, which I guess they'd had my assistant pull together. Their approach was very clever: you couldn't say, "I can't start right now because I need such and such" because anything you could think of had already been provided. So you were kind of backed into a corner.

The next day I was called back to the admissions office, where I found Joel Schumacher and the two producers of the movie. It hadn't occurred to me that they were behind all this. What could it matter to them if they had *me* in their film? First of all, I was nobody. This was only my third studio movie. And, what's more, there were seven of us in the cast—what difference did I really make? But they had apparently met to discuss the situation because there was a negotiated plan in place. I could start the film with just fifteen days of sobriety if I completed the list of requirements that are usually done in thirty. When I left, there had to be a counselor with me 24/7 for the duration of the filming.

To this day, I see this as some version of divine intervention. If I'd had to give up the movie and go through the program to get sober for *myself*, I doubt I would have done it. I just didn't value myself enough for that. But with the film at stake, and this enormous show of support from Craig Baumgarten, Joel Schumacher, and his colleagues, who I didn't want to let down, I had something much bigger than me to fight for. And so I did.

I did absolutely everything that was asked of me. I checked every requirement off the list. I cooperated. I worked hard. I went to group counseling and one-on-one counseling, and I went to AA meetings and accepted the twelve steps into my life. There was even a family session, which my mother and brother attended. I got to vent my grievances at Ginny, but even in this environment it was clear she wasn't capable of mothering me. So I just went through the motions and got it over with. It's sort of funny to think about me apologizing for any problems I might have caused her because of *my* addiction.

Fifteen days later, I walked out with my wonderful, caring counselor and went straight to rehearsal. True to the conditions of my release from the rehab, she stayed with me day and night while we filmed at various locations in Washington, D.C., and around the campus at the University of Maryland, which we pretended was Georgetown. She was a lovely woman, a maternal presence that I hadn't had since I'd lived with my grandmother in Roswell. Once again, I had that precious, reassuring feeling that someone was looking out for me, that someone cared about how I was doing. Schumacher—to his credit—just moved on, focusing on me as a professional, which was the most helpful thing he could possibly have done. Obviously, both Craig and Joel did an amazingly generous thing by supporting me while I got sober.

Sobriety was still anonymous back then—no one was admitting to, let alone trumpeting, going to rehab, and I did my best to keep a low profile and just be part of the group as we were shooting. Besides the seven of us, there were other young actors—around that set and at the parties we had when we finished shooting—who had been in films with different members of the cast: Molly Ringwald, Matt Dillon, Sean Penn and his brother Chris. We were dubbed the Brat Pack in the press, a term I *hated*, because it implied we were all a bunch of spoiled, partying, entitled juvenile delinquents. I'd never been anything even close to spoiled, and I certainly wasn't partying.

Once I made the decision to get clean and sober, staying that way was actually easy. The negotiation was over: I never wanted to experience that moment of waking up and trying to remember what I had done the night before again. I didn't want any more of that embarrassment. I wanted to be present, not dulled by alcohol or sped up by cocaine, and I dedicated myself fully to the process. I'd always been interested in spirituality but felt uninspired by organized religion. Once I saw that the principles of AA were centered on trusting God "as we understand Him," I knew I had found a point of connection.

AA also helped me understand more about my parents. One of the program's many catchphrases is "doing a geographic," meaning when people like my mom and dad pick up and move instead of dealing with their shit head-on—not realizing, of course, that they are always *taking their shit with them.* "If you do what you've always done, you'll get what you've always gotten" is another AA slogan that struck home with me, because it perfectly encapsulated my parents' approach to life, and the inevitably disappointing outcomes they ended up with, over and over again.

St. Elmo's Fire got passable reviews. The *New York Times* called it "as good a film as any to put into a time capsule this year to show what and whom young viewers want." It did all right at the box office, too. Ultimately, it became a kind of classic of the era, a quintessential coming-of-age movie, and it definitely gave my career a massive boost.

But for me personally, *St. Elmo's* will always be the movie that changed my life. If I hadn't gone to rehab to make that film, I really wonder if I'd still be alive. And while I didn't really think, *Holy shit! I'm in a hit!* at the time, I did have a tingly feeling that something had struck.

CHAPTER 10

Emilio and I started dating seriously after I got sober. We were together for six months, and then we got engaged, and I moved in with him in his condo in Malibu. He was very sweet, very attentive, and, looking back, I think a major factor in how quickly we moved was that I was craving a family, and he had a close relationship with his. They lived nearby and, in fact, when I first met Emilio, he was still living at home with his mother, Janet, an artist; his father, Martin Sheen (whose birth name was Ramón Estévez); his little sister, Renée; and his brothers, Ramón Estévez and Charlie Sheen, who'd taken his father's stage name. All of the members of the Sheen/Estevez family were actors except for Janet, and whereas I'd always thought of acting as a job, they considered it an art form. I hung on to their every word, trying to absorb some of their seriousness and passion.

Martin had reembraced Catholicism after suffering a heart attack at thirty-six, and had subsequently overcome his own alcoholism. That was an inspiration to me. Emilio's mom, Janet, had a no-nonsense side, and she was the pillar of the family. I particularly liked Charlie, who I saw as extremely bright and quick-witted, but also as an artist who was full of emotion. He showed me some of his poetry, and I remember being struck by the intensity of his feelings. That was the part of Charlie that a lot of people perhaps didn't see, or maybe still haven't—a more gentle, fragile, emotional man than the cocky, combative persona he has projected publicly. Look back at his performance in *Platoon*: that didn't come out of nowhere.

Emilio and I would often go over to the family house to have dinner or hang out on the weekends. I never really felt fully incorporated into their clan, but I'm sure that had much more to do with me than with them. (I've seen his mother since and talked to her, and she had a totally different perspective of me than I would have thought.) I, of course, assumed that I wasn't good enough for them—not educated or smart or sophisticated enough. I'd never known people with such strong principles, especially Martin. A longtime political activist, he had been arrested for his anti-war stance, at anti-nuclear demonstrations, for supporting Cesar Chavez, and so on. I was fascinated by all of it but rarely joined in the political discussions at their table, feeling I had everything to learn and little to contribute.

Emilio and his family were, in a lot of ways, a good influence on me. He hated cigarettes, so I gave them up. Unfortunately, like a lot of people quitting smoking, I started putting on weight once I didn't have the crutch of my cigarettes. It became a problem in the summer of 1985, when I got cast in the movie *One Crazy Summer*, which required me to be in a bathing suit much of the time. We shot on the beach in Massachusetts, on Cape Cod and Nantucket. It was a dream setting for a truly wacky comedy with some very wild comedic actors: John Cusack, Curtis Armstrong, and the legendary William Hickey. I was pretty much the only girl, which was kind of isolating, until I met a quirky, wonderful social worker who was on the set to work with the kids in the movie. Her name was Patsy Rugg, and she became one of the pivotal people in my life.

We got talking the way women do, and when it emerged that I was newly sober, she told me that she had been sober herself for a very long time. She offered to be my sponsor. Her generosity and guidance made all the difference in the world. All of a sudden, I had a support system, someone I could count on. Patsy didn't have kids, but she certainly was a mother to me.

But I was having serious food issues. I could barely bring myself to look in a mirror during the filming of *One Crazy Summer* because I hated what I saw and worried about how it would translate on-screen. I was also frightened; I was sure any director would find my shape unacceptable and I'd never get another part.

This was very much on my mind when my new agent, Paula Wagner at CAA, told me I had landed an audition for a romantic comedy called *About Last Night*. We were still shooting *One*

Crazy Summer; I had a head full of beachy braids when I went in to read for Debbie, the lead, and I had to explain to the director, Ed Zwick, that it wasn't my usual look. He hadn't yet cast the male lead, but Ed said he liked me for the part of Debbie, and we had a very good meeting. I was nervous but excited about the prospect of my first major role in a big movie.

The casting process seemed to move at a snail's pace, and I grew anxious waiting, especially after I learned that he'd hired my old pal Rob Lowe. It seemed like it made more sense to cast me now than ever. But a full month went by. Finally, Ed Zwick called. When I went in to see him at his office in L.A., my worst nightmare came true: he sat down and said, "You are really who I would like to do this film, but you would have to promise me that you would lose weight." I'll never forget that moment as long as I live. I felt a combination of sick, pit-of-my-stomach mortification and raw panic. And so began my process of trying to dominate and control my body—and of equating my worth to my weight, my size, my exterior.

In fairness to Ed, I was not leading-lady thin. I'm not tall, and I have a delicate frame, and I *had* gained weight—whether it was fifteen pounds or twenty, on me, it was a lot. If I'd had better self-esteem, it easily could have been different; I could have simply said, "You know what? You're right: I gained a little bit of weight, and I can lose that." And on the outside, of course, that's exactly how I handled it. I said, "I absolutely see it; I'll do whatever it takes because I'm totally committed to doing the film." (And I *was* totally committed: I knew what it meant to have a big part in a studio film, one I rightly believed could be a hit.) But I did not approach the issue in a rational, healthy way. I was thrown into a tailspin of terror and self-loathing.

I was sober, sure, but all my anxieties just shifted over to food. If I got on a scale, it could ruin my entire day. I have journals upon journals from that period, full of writing about my pain and torture over my body. I'd wake up in the middle of the night and binge-eat and then be covered in crumbs in the morning. I even put a lock on my refrigerator door at one point. It was like food had become a weapon to use in a war against my body, the enemy. I used food as a kind of punishment for everything I believed was wrong and dirty about myself: I imbued it with every bad feeling, all my shame, and then gobbled it up.

With drugs or alcohol or cigarettes, it's a basic yes or no—either you use them, or you don't. Yes or no is straightforward. I'm not saying quitting is easy, but in my experience, once the negotiation is off the table, it's just a *no*, and then you can deal with the feelings that arise from it. Once I wrapped my head around the idea that partying simply wasn't an option for me, then it was a different ball game. But with food, you can't do that. You *have* to eat. I remember somebody saying, it's like having a lion that you have to take out for a walk three times a day.

For *years*, I couldn't figure out how to eat. It didn't help that because of my kidney disease, there was damage to my intestines and problems with my metabolism from having taken high levels of steroids as a kid. They saved my life, but they also wreaked total havoc on my digestive system. But the problem wasn't just physiological: as I have since come to realize, I had never learned how to digest *emotionally*. I'd never learned how to take something like disappointment or rejection and really break it down, metabolize it, digest it.

If *One Crazy Summer* put my body on display in a bathing suit, *About Last Night* upped the ante. Based on the David Mamet play *Sexual Perversity in Chicago*, *About Last Night* was, for its time, a daring movie: my character, Debbie, and Rob's character, Danny, meet at a singles' bar and have what they think will be a one-night stand; the next morning, Debbie basically flees. Remember: this was way before *Sex and the City*. The idea that a woman would just want to get laid and then bail without trying to start a relationship was radical. There were a lot of sex scenes, which meant I had to spend a great deal of time naked in front of a room full of men: camera operators, producers, sound guys, and the director who'd told me I was too fat to be in a film.

It's telling that when Rob and Ed reminisced about the film—which became a huge hit—many years later for the release of the DVD, Rob remembered the two of us being close to hypothermia in a scene shot outdoors in freezing weather and, in another scene, the pain he was in when his leg gave out while he was carrying me. For my part, I just remember the agony I was in displaying my body for the world to see.

Fortunately, the cast was very friendly and supportive, and we all got along well. I'd never worked before with Jim Belushi or with Elizabeth Perkins, who was making her movie debut, but there was a wonderful camaraderie on the set. Rob and I were old friends, and he and Emilio were also close, having grown up together in Malibu, so there were definite boundaries in the sex scenes I had with Rob that made them easier to shoot. But the self-consciousness I felt about my body was almost paralyzing.

About Last Night was released on July 2, 1986, and pulled in over $38 million. It got decent reviews for the most part, and so did I. Roger Ebert wrote in the *Chicago Sun-Times*: "Moore is especially impressive. There isn't a romantic note she isn't required to play in this movie, and she plays them all flawlessly." No critics remarked on my horrible body, which should have proven to me that my horrible body was all in my head.

NEXT, I WENT to do my one and only play in New York, *The Early Girl*, off-Broadway. The part required me to run onstage completely naked, night after night, in front of a live audience. (The play centered on prostitutes at a Nevada brothel.) Clearly something in me was attracting these kinds of roles. I easily could have said no, but on a deeper level I knew that I needed to be pushed out of my comfort zone—that if I was ever going to overcome my body issues, I had to confront them head-on.

The Early Girl was playing at the Circle Rep downtown, and my agents found me an apartment at one of the first Trump apartment buildings on Fifth Avenue. I threw myself a twenty-third birthday party there, and I dared to invite Andy Warhol, whom I'd met one night at Indochine. I was amazed to read years later in *The Andy Warhol Diaries* that not only had Andy been to see the play, but felt that he had "got Demi Moore to invite me to her wedding."

Emilio and I had in fact just mailed out the invitations for our wedding when a friend told me she had seen him out with someone else in L.A. He denied it, of course, but I was having a hard time trusting him: during a two-week breakup a few months before, he'd slept with an "ex" girlfriend, lied about it, and then been forced to tell me the truth when he found out she was pregnant. On my one day a week off from the play, I started going up to Boston to see a therapist who'd been recommended to me by my sponsor Patsy.

I remember the therapist saying to me after a few sessions, "Ordinarily I prefer for a patient to come to an understanding on her own. But I don't have time to let that happen, so I just have to tell you: if you marry him the way things are right now, you're going to ruin your life." She suggested Emilio come in for a session. She wanted him to communicate his priorities to me directly, in person. He was resistant, but he finally did make the trip, and when he revealed his priorities in that session— you'll be shocked to hear—I was pretty low on the list. I postponed the wedding indefinitely.

When the play had finished its run, I went back to California, but soon after I returned, Emilio went to Canada to do a film—*Stakeout*, with Richard Dreyfuss. I remember trying to reach him and him not answering the phone, and just *knowing* it meant more than that he was busy working. He didn't want me to come up there to talk in person, either, and that's when I thought, *You know what? I'm going to stop trying to call him and call a realtor instead.*

I found an adorable fifties beach house on the end of a cul-de-sac in Malibu. And then I told Emilio I was moving out. He showed up in no time with a tattoo of a broken heart, trying to get me back. I think he was one of those men, at least in his youth, who found you much more interesting once he'd lost you. But it was too late: once I'm done, I'm done.

We stayed friends, though, and I went with Emilio to the premiere of *Stakeout* a few months after we broke up. It turned out to be a highly consequential night in my life, because at that premiere, I met an actor who was very hot at the time, on a hit series called *Moonlighting*. His name was Bruce Willis.

CHAPTER 11

He's all over you, like a cheap suit in the rain," Emilio said, of the cocky, dark, and handsome guy who'd been introduced to me as Bruce Willis. Actually, I'd thought Bruce was dismissive at first. He happened to walk into the premiere at the same time I did, and he was with a friend of mine, the comedian Rick Ducommun, who introduced us. Bruce had already been nominated for an Emmy for *Moonlighting* twice by then (he would win the award the next month), but I didn't watch much television and had never seen the show—my only familiarity with his work was from one of those Seagram's Golden Wine Cooler commercials he used to do. (Remember those? He'd blow a few bluesy chords on the harmonica and wail, "It's wet and it's dry! My, my, my.") We both had deals with TriStar Pictures, so I said, "I hear you have the good office at TriStar."

He replied with something short, like, "I'm never there." My impression was, he's kind of a jerk.

But when I saw him at the after-party at El Coyote, Bruce was suddenly much more solicitous. "Hey, can I buy you a drink?" he asked, as soon as I walked in. I told him I didn't drink. "Well let me buy you a Perrier," he countered. Bruce—who'd been a bartender in New York City before he became a television star—was showing off behind the bar that night, tossing the cocktail shaker in the air, the kind of thing that seemed cool in 1987 but sounds cringeworthy now, and Emilio had a point: Bruce was looking at me a *lot* as he went through his bar moves. He was so attentive as the evening progressed, I was stunned to find out later that he'd actually been on a date that night with another woman!

When it got late, people were going to see Rick Ducommun do a stand-up set at the Improv. "You should come! You should come!" Bruce and Rick implored me. I could see Emilio wasn't thrilled by all the attention they were paying to me—I wish I'd been a little less thrilled myself. But the club was on my way home anyway, so I figured I'd stop by. When I got there, I could see all of Bruce's buddies sitting at a big table. Next to them, Bruce had set a table for two, with a Perrier waiting for me. He jumped up and pulled out my chair.

I'd never encountered treatment like this before. Bruce was so gallant—in his own boisterous way, a real gentleman. When I said it was time for me to go home, he offered to walk me to my car. He was so eager about it—like a little boy who didn't want to miss the ice-cream truck. When he asked for my number, I felt a wave of schoolgirl flutters. "Do you have a pen?" He checked his pockets and came up empty. "Don't leave!" he said, and went skittering off to get one. Then he wrote it on his arm—a sight I'd see a million times over the years; Bruce was always writing things on his arm. But that first time, I noticed that his hands were shaking. He was so vulnerable in that moment: all of the bravado was gone.

I drove home replaying the events of the night. *What just happened?* I wondered. *Who is this guy?* I was trying to add up all the information that had just come at me. (This was before cell phones; it's not like I could call around asking people about him.) I'd never actually had anyone ask me out on a real date before. I'd met Freddy through the music scene and Emilio on set; the relationships I'd had up to this point had just sort of happened through proximity and flirtation. But this did not feel like a pickup—this was not somebody who was trying to add a notch to his belt.

Bruce was so dynamic. One thing he's never had a problem with is taking his space. (He's definitely never asked, Is it okay that I'm here?) I felt a pang of concern for Emilio—even though he had invited me as "his friend" that evening, I was aware that he had hopes of repairing our romance.

Fifteen minutes later, I was cruising down the Pacific Coast Highway toward my new house in Malibu, all the way out past Point Dume. To my right were the mountains and the stars, to my left was the moonlit ocean. Everything was peaceful. I thought about Emilio; I thought about Bruce. And then I could swear I heard my name in the wind. No, it wasn't my dad visiting from the spirit world: it was a stretch limousine in the next lane, with Bruce Willis and his buddies poking up through the open sunroof, waving and shouting, "Hey, Demi!" (This was before the days of the ever-present black SUVs ferrying celebrities everywhere. When Bruce was partying, he'd hire a limo to take him and his friends out for the night in style.) I couldn't believe I was looking out my window at the guy I'd just been thinking about. It was like the universe was telling me: pay attention to this one.

Bruce flipped his baseball cap off to salute me when our eyes met, and I guess he'd forgotten he'd stashed a joint behind each ear because they went flying into the night.

HE CALLED ME first thing the next morning. He asked what I was doing that day, and I told him I was driving to Orange County to see George and DeAnna. "I'll go with you," he told me, to my surprise. I wasn't entirely sure this was a good idea. My dad's sister Mary was visiting them, and she was a *true* character. "My kooky aunt is going to be there, and it's a very small house," I said. "Are you sure?" He was sure.

Again, I was impressed. This was a guy who was going to spend two hours in a car just for the dubious pleasure of meeting my weird relatives. He was willing to put himself out of his comfort zone, and he was doing something that was *purely* for me. Honestly, I found it shocking.

His house, which was right on the beach, was on the way, so I went by to pick him up. All of his buddies were still there from the night before—they traveled as a pack around Los Angeles, partying, hanging out, and meeting girls. They were like the eighties version of *Entourage*, but they were good-spirited and fun: they used to call themselves the New Rat Pack. I met John Goodman that morning, and Woody Harrelson, who was on *Cheers* at the time, both of whom would become good friends. Bruce waved goodbye to his posse, and off we went.

It was a fun ride. It's hard not to feel good when someone showers you with that much attention. I think Bruce saw me as some kind of angelic savior when we first met, I don't really know why—maybe partly because I was sober and not a party girl. He hung on my words and didn't bat an eye once we got to Orange County and he met my nutty aunt. "We're from Neeeeeew Mexico!" was the first thing out of her mouth. Bruce just rolled with it. George and DeAnna got a kick out of him; he was cut from the same cloth as the men in our family: charismatic, mischievous, with a little twinkle in his eye. A charming ladies' man with a great sense of humor, like my father and my granddaddy (much more so than I realized at the time).

The next night he took me downtown to see a Shakespeare play that John Goodman was in (if I remember correctly, most of the New Rat Pack were with us on that date). Basically, from that first meeting on, Bruce and I were rarely apart. He made me feel like a princess; he lived large—and soon I did, too. Bruce came from nothing, and now that he'd made it, he wanted the best of everything, and plenty of it. We would go to a restaurant, and he would order three entrées and have a few bites of each, just because he could. He loved to gamble. He relished the power that money has to wipe away obstacles. Years later, at three in the morning, when one of the babies was crying, he would lean over and whisper, "I'll give you a thousand dollars if you change that diaper."

Bruce, having worked in Manhattan at Café Centro, which was a real hot spot at the time, knew all the "in" restaurants and clubs, and he enjoyed exposing me to a world of perks that was totally new. Not long after we met we flew on a private plane to see his band perform at a fairground—it was my first time on a small jet. *A girl could get used to this*, I thought.

A few weeks later, he took me to London. It was a whirlwind, my first time in Europe. I'd never had jet lag before, and when we went to dinner our first night, I felt like I'd been run over by a truck and didn't understand what was wrong with me. And the paparazzi in London were on a whole different level—for one thing, they were allowed in the airport. They were waiting for us when we landed, and they didn't let up the entire time we were in England. I'd never experienced anything like it before. We were stalked, hounded—I remember one time a photographer literally ran down the street after Bruce. He had the ability to just barrel on, but I would have been happier to stay at the hotel. I was totally unprepared for that creepy, besieged feeling.

It gets a little easier when you know what to expect, but then? I was shell-shocked. To be honest, when we got on the plane to go home, I was relieved.

It was a taste of what was to come. One day not long after we returned from London, we were hanging out by the beach at Bruce's house with his friends, and I took his Jet Ski out for a spin. Someone with a long lens got pictures of me in a bathing suit—looking fat—which then, of course, became a major topic in the tabloids, confirming all my worst fears and stoking the excruciating fire of my eating disorder. I was miserable, but Bruce insisted that he thought everything about me was beautiful: he wrapped my fear and anxiety in his love.

When Bruce and I got together, our traumas met. Bruce had had a difficult childhood: he was a stutterer, which had the positive side effect of getting him into acting. For some reason, kids who stutter often find themselves freed of their speech impediment when they are onstage, reciting lines instead of coming up with words in real time. So Bruce and I had both grown up performing, role-playing for survival.

He was the oldest of four, the son of a very hardworking immigrant mother who was never appreciated by her husband. They divorced, and years later, the dad mellowed, as men tend to when they get older. (You know the kind: they're assholes when they're young, then they get sweet when they age; it's the mother who seems bitter and unpleasant by comparison, but he's the one who made her that way.)

I imagine it would be difficult to see the wounded kid under

Bruce's roguish exterior if you didn't know him. But believe me, it's there. I understood that about him immediately. We went all in, right away—talking about how badly we both wanted to have kids, our own family. We had a shared vision for our future. I think we were both longing to fill the emptiness, that sense we'd both always had that something big was missing.

Bruce was on hiatus from *Moonlighting* when we first met, and I had just finished making *The Seventh Sign*. We were able to spend almost all our time together until he started shooting an action movie he was really excited about: *Die Hard*. There was a lot of buzz about the film, in large part because it was reported that Bruce got paid $5 million to star in it. I went to see him on set, which turned out to be terrifying. He nearly died jumping off a five-story garage, just making it onto the airbag below when he was blown off course by a scripted explosion. (He laughed about it. I didn't.)

When he got a weekend off from filming, he took me to Vegas on another private jet to see a fight—he loved boxing. It was Chavez versus Rosario, and it was hideous. Rosario's trainer had to stop the fight. I don't mind boxing, but I don't like a bloodbath.

We were moving to the gambling tables when Bruce said, "I think we should get married." We'd been joking about it on the flight there, but suddenly it didn't seem like he was kidding. "I think we should get married," he said again. I was speechless. He, on the other hand, wouldn't stop talking: "Come on, let's do it! Let's do it." I took a deep breath and said, "Okay let's do it."

I got pregnant on my wedding night, November 21, 1987, at the Golden Nugget. (Yes: Vegas. Pregnant. You can take the girl out of Roswell, but apparently you can't take Roswell out of the girl.)

We decided to have a real wedding about a month later, and that became a huge production. It was TriStar's gift to us: they understood the once-in-a-lifetime publicity opportunity they had on their hands. Bruce was on the verge of transforming from TV heartthrob into full-on international movie star, and they had high hopes for me, too, after *About Last Night* was a major hit. Our second wedding was as lavish and over the top as our first one was ad hoc. It was held on the soundstages on the Warner Bros. lot, and they borrowed a staircase from *Designing Women* so I could make a grand entrance into the "chapel," where we had set up traditional church-style seating. Little Richard performed the ceremony. ("DahMEE, do you take this man to be your lawfully wedded husband, whether he live in a big mansion on the hill or a little tiny apartment?") Annie Leibovitz was the photographer. The bridesmaids wore black and entered with the groomsmen singing "Bruno's Getting Married," written for the occasion by Bruce's good friend Robert Kraft. Afterward, we went to a second soundstage for the reception, which had been done up with palm trees in the style of the Copacabana. It should have been a blast, one of the great, shining days of my life. But in truth it was overwhelming. Both of Bruce's parents came—the first time they'd been in the same room since they'd divorced—George and DeAnna were there, of course, and my grandmother flew in from New Mexico with her beau, Harold (though when I first told her I had gotten together with Bruce, she was worried because she'd read in the tabloids he was a wild party boy). My mom came, too, for better or worse.

Ginny made a scene, of course, while she was in town for the wedding. She was staying at my house, and Bruce and I were at his place on our (second) wedding night, when the phone rang at two a.m. It was the police, calling to report a disturbance. I honestly can't recall the details—there were so many incidents like this they all blur together in my memory—but suffice it to say that Ginny was wasted and had managed to start a fight with my neighbors, a fight dramatic enough to require cops to intervene. I was furious at her for failing, just this once, to hold it together for my sake.

Bruce grasped the deal with my mom right away, and understood that where Ginny was concerned, the more boundaries we put in place, the better. Very soon, I would need a model for how to be a mother, and while I continued to hold out false hope that someday, somehow, she'd step up, that obviously wasn't something I could count on.

RUMER GLENN WILLIS was born on her due date, August 16, 1988, in Paducah, Kentucky, where Bruce was shooting a movie called *In Country*. I wanted the exact opposite experience to the one my mom had: I wanted to feel every sensation, to be completely present and conscious for every moment of the delivery, no matter how painful. I had to switch doctors at the last minute to find one who appreciated my approach: "Same with my cows," he assured me. "They never need episiotomies." Rumer spent the first half hour of her life alone with just Bruce and me in the hospital bed, as we both fell madly in love with our daughter. Then I got up, took a shower, and we left the hospital.

She was named after the British author Rumer Godden, whose name I came upon in a bookstore one day while I was having trouble coming up with the perfect, one-of-a-kind name for my first baby. I had loved being pregnant. The whole experience was wonderful from beginning to end. It didn't hurt that Bruce was constantly telling me how beautiful I looked for nine months.

Being a mother felt totally natural. It's one of the few things I can confidently say I was innately good at. Nurturing Rumer, having someone to love who loved and needed me right back, unconditionally, exactly as I was, without any kind of performance, was euphoric. It would be over two years before I left Rumer for even a single night—two years of breastfeeding her.

Even my messed-up relationship with my own mother seemed transformed by the birth of my daughter: Ginny came and spent a week with us after Rumer was born, and I can't remember ever having a nicer time together. It was almost like she, too, was able to shut out all the outside things in her life that weren't working and devote herself totally to this experience. She fussed over the baby and took lots of photographs—did all the things a normal grandmother would do. By the time she left, I felt more like Ginny and I were mother and daughter than I had since I was very small. Sometimes I wonder if I should have invited her to live with us and take on the role of full-time grandmother—if it would have redirected her life and given her the sense of purpose, security, and fulfillment that she needed so badly.

I was twenty-five. I had a lot more maturity under my belt than Ginny did when she had me at eighteen, but I was still young. Life had bounced from one enormous event to the next in a very rapid succession. One minute I was planning my wedding; the next I was shopping for baby clothes. Bruce and I were becoming the "It" couple; we had the blessing of a beautiful, healthy little girl, and we had more money than either of us knew to wish for as kids.

I know that sounds like the perfect life. But as I would soon find out, if you carry a well of shame and unresolved trauma inside of you, no amount of money, no measure of success or celebrity, can fill it.

CHAPTER 12

Soon after we met, Bruce had bought a property in Idaho's Wood River Valley, in a town called Hailey. He'd broken his collarbone in a skiing accident in nearby Sun Valley, and while he was hanging around recuperating, he fell in love with the quiet, the big sky, and the indifference the locals seemed to display toward anything Hollywood-related. I loved it there right away, too. We completely renovated the original house—only the front door remains—and ever since I've spent as much time in Idaho as possible, especially with my kids. It became my oasis, the place where I felt more at home than I ever have anywhere else—I still do. There is something about being surrounded by the Sawtooth Mountains, where the air is clear and cool, and there's almost no noise at all except for the fast current of the Big Wood River, that soothes me and gives me a sense of peace. Rumer was only twelve days old when we took her to

Hailey for the first time. The early weeks and months of her life there were wondrous for me.

But four months after that great visit with my mother and the baby, I got a call from the police: Ginny had overdosed on pills and had been rushed to the hospital. She was okay, but a few months after that, I got another call: she had been arrested for drunk driving. She was obviously coming apart, so I checked her into rehab.

The first thing she did when she got out was to sell a story to a tabloid about her recovery . . . and our troubled relationship.

I was furious. Understand, I *hated* the tabloids. Having paparazzi chase you around probably doesn't sound like that big a deal. Before they were a part of my life, I'm sure I would have shrugged and said, "So what?," if I read about the combination of horror, terror, and rage an actress felt just because a bunch of guys were always taking her picture. But try to think of it like this: You know that wonderful feeling you get once in a while when you have an hour to yourself and none of your kids or clients or parents need anything from you and you don't have to answer the phone and you can just walk out your front door—or pull out of your driveway—and blend into the world? When the tabloids are stalking you, those moments never, ever happen. Having paparazzi always waiting to pounce on you like wild dogs—unreasonable, menacing, solely interested in what they can *take*—can start to feel invasive on an almost existential level.

That's a long way of saying I asked Ginny not to do that

again. I tried to explain what a violation it was to share details (and falsehoods) about my childhood with publications that are in the business of lying, sensationalizing, and exploiting. Ginny agreed, but then she started selling pictures of me instead. Obviously, she didn't quite get the larger point. I have a copy of one of the letters from her "agent," pitching the rights to some pictures of me to magazines in Italy, Australia, Germany, Spain, Britain, and France: "Demi Moore's mother has finally opened the family album to uncover her superstar daughter's photo secrets!" it says, and then describes eighteen never-before-published pictures, including one from my wedding to Freddy, which the letter claims I had "tried to hide." It also mentions a photo from my wedding with Bruce, a snapshot of Bruce and me in a Jacuzzi, and a picture of me as a kid in a hospital bed, captioned "the day she nearly died." Ginny and her agent were asking for ten thousand dollars per country.

I persuaded her to hold back a picture of Rumer she was going to send in, and the photo of Bruce in the hot tub, but I couldn't talk her out of selling the rest of them, which gutted me. What she was doing for money was feeding something I spent a tremendous amount of time and energy keeping out of our lives. To this day, I still make extra efforts to think about where I'm going and what access the paparazzi will have and what my comfort level with that is. If I take that caution and multiply it a hundredfold, that's how I felt when Rumer— and later her sisters—were little. I wanted to protect my daughters from everything invasive and ugly; it was one of the main reasons we ended up raising our girls in Idaho, not California. I think it's one of the best decisions Bruce and I ever made.

The fact that Ginny wouldn't recognize that what she was doing was a complete betrayal; she knew full well how I felt about those magazines and the lies they had printed about me in the past.

I know: the only thing that's surprising about all this is that *I* was—yet again—surprised. Children are hardwired to trust their parents. It's amazing just how long it can take to override that wiring.

I HAD DECIDED that after my pregnancy, my body would be better than ever. I looked at it as an opportunity to hit the reset button. Within three months, I'd lost all the pregnancy weight, plus another eight pounds. I was invited to host *Saturday Night Live* right around then, and the writers actually got me to base my whole opening monologue around the line, "I had a baby just twelve weeks ago, and *look* at me!" I was never comfortable with that conceit, but at that time I didn't have the confidence to push back. They were like, "Trust us, it's going to work!" And it could have, if I'd really been able to own it and commit to the bit. I just didn't know how to embrace saying "Don't I look great?" enough for it to be funny. Performing that monologue was torture. It was terrifying enough getting in front of a live audience and essentially doing stand-up comedy, and honestly, I was afraid the joke was on me. All the negative talk in my head really stole that experience from me, and I didn't fully inhabit my time with the amazing performers who were in the cast that season: Dana Carvey, Jon Lovitz, Phil Hartman, Nora Dunn, and Al Franken. *SNL* moves fast—I remember at the end of the show, when we were saying good night to the audience, *that's* when I finally felt, *Okay, I got this now. Let's do the whole thing over again for real!*

Not long after I did *SNL*, I was offered a movie with Robert De Niro and Sean Penn called *We're No Angels*, a comedy. It would be directed by Neil Jordan, an Irishman whose films *Mona Lisa* and *High Spirits* I'd admired, and the idea that I might be in a film with those actors was exhilarating. If I was good enough to work with people of that caliber, I told myself, how bad could I be?

It felt like a turning point, an indication that maybe it was time to trust myself more as an actor. Bruce's reaction to the opportunity was not what I would have hoped, however. I remember distinctly being in the bedroom, changing Rumer's diaper and telling Bruce what an amazing project this was going to be, how excited I was to shoot a film in Canada with *the* Robert De Niro. Bruce's expression was stony as he said: "This will never work."

I was baffled. "What do you mean, this won't work?" I genuinely didn't understand what he was talking about.

"This is never going to work," he continued, "if you're off shooting a film." What he meant was that *our life* wouldn't work if I was engrossed in something outside of our family.

I was taken aback. It's not like it was a secret what we both did for a living before we started a family—Bruce understood from the inside what my job entailed, and I assumed that he expected me to keep on doing it. But in the very short time we'd known each other before getting married, I'd only been doing press and other ancillary aspects of my job, not actually working full time on a movie: my work hadn't involved any demands that took me away from prioritizing *him*. In that moment, while I was changing that diaper, it was like a whole other side of his perspective and mine met for the very first time. I felt panic mounting. "Well, we'll *make it* work," I told him, and shifted into solution-oriented mode. I assured him that the schedule had been set up so I could easily bring Rumer with me, and I'd go back and forth to spend time with him. I felt *way* too much anxiety to have a real conversation with Bruce about our assumptions regarding work, gender roles, and parenting—the deep stuff we obviously needed to start figuring out together to have a successful marriage. Instead, I jumped right into "How can I fix this?" and started frantically figuring out what it would take to accommodate Bruce's work schedule—and his expectations.

Rumer was five months old when I took her with me to shoot *We're No Angels*, and I flew home with her every weekend. I think Bruce came to us once. It was difficult. I was not my most confident with the work, and I did not have the support of somebody saying "Of course you can do this." I had to cheerlead for myself, and for the relationship.

It was inspiring acting alongside Penn and De Niro, but there was bad chemistry on the set—Sean and the director didn't exactly see eye to eye. The film wasn't a commercial success. But my next movie, thank goodness, would make up for that.

GHOST WAS AN unusual script. There was the romance between the protagonists, so deep that it transcended even death. There was a murder and the quest for the killer's real motivation. And then there was a whole funny side story involving a shady psychic hustler. Really, it was three movies in one: a love story, a thriller, and a comedy. And with an unknown commodity attached, the director Jerry Zucker. He'd had a hit with the hilarious classic *Airplane!* but had never attempted anything quite like this.

I had a deep interest in the spiritual aspect of the story, the connection we all have with what is beyond our ordinary senses, so I was over the moon about that aspect of the script. But I knew that with so many elements in play, it was a risky film to do. When I read *Ghost* I thought, *This could be either an absolute disaster or it could be amazing.*

I didn't have to audition for the part of Molly Jensen, the female lead; they'd seen my other movies and they wanted me for this one, which was flattering. I met with Jerry and the producers, once in L.A. and once when Bruce, Rumer, and I stopped in New York on our way to Paris, where we were going for our first real vacation as a family. I was determined to get my hair cut short while I was there—I had a picture of Isabella Rossellini looking boyishly chic in my wallet to show my fantasy Parisian stylist. I still hadn't made up my mind whether to do *Ghost*, so I felt free to do whatever I wanted with my look.

I'd never been to Paris before, and I didn't speak a word of French. But I was a woman with a mission: I walked around the corner from the apartment we were renting on the Left Bank to the first salon I saw, and showed them the picture of Isabella in all her sophisticated, short-haired glory. This was Paris, after all, I figured—they knew about style, of course they could do it.

Turns out they couldn't. The cut, though short, was not at all what I had in mind. Funnily enough, when we got home, I went to see a hairdresser a friend recommended: he took one look at the picture of Isabella Rossellini and said, "I did that haircut." And then he fixed me right up. I loved it. That haircut did exactly what I'd hoped: it gave me a whole new look and made me feel revived and emboldened. There was something fresh and unexpected about it.

Jerry Zucker was shocked—and, I'm pretty sure, horrified—when I met up with him after we got back and told him I had decided to make the movie. He had cast Patrick Swayze to play the protagonist Sam Wheat, and as his girlfriend he'd chosen an actress with long, flowing dark hair: instead, he suddenly had someone with practically no hair at all. But Jerry went with it and didn't make me wear a wig, and personally I think the short hair suited the character perfectly.

Molly was supposed to be an artist, living a bohemian life in Tribeca—the old Tribeca of the eighties, a land of artists scraping by in lofts, though, presciently, her boyfriend, Sam, was in finance, as so many of Tribeca's inhabitants are today. Jerry had a very particular vision in mind. He took Patrick and me to see the loft he was picturing in New York; he felt it said everything about this couple's relationship and their style. The set designers at Paramount re-created that loft down to the last detail for us back in L.A. To me this has always been one of the most miraculous parts of the movie industry: that a director can show his team his mom's kitchen, for instance, and tell them "This is what I want," and then off they go and create its double as if by magic. When we got to the set and saw the "loft" they had constructed, it was *exactly* like the one Jerry had found in Tribeca, from the creaky floorboards to the tall windows.

Molly's primary art form was ceramics, and they hired a potter to teach me how to use a wheel. I went quite a few times to practice throwing these teeny, tiny little pots, which I still have. They are very amateurish, of course, but they remind me of what a singular experience it was, meeting the artist whose work we used in the movie as Molly's. She had such passion about her craft, and a real ease with the clay. I soon discovered that the smallest pressure could transform—and destroy—the shape you were making on the wheel, and there I was, faking it on film. It was especially challenging pulling off the scene when Patrick joined me behind the potter's wheel, and both of our hands were molding the clay as it grew taller and taller, until it was basically a giant clay erection—in danger of collapsing.

The other anxiety-inducing aspect of that movie was much more profound. Reading the script, I'd recognized the level of emotion that was going to be required: not hysterical sobbing kinds of scenes, but rather scenes that were quietly intense, the hardest kind. I remembered Emilio and his family talking about actors crying, and how they often scrunched up their faces, which made their tears seem forced and fake. But I didn't know if I could cry at all—and I don't mean just as an actor. I didn't cry off-screen, either. Ever. I had learned to bottle myself up to get by, and I wasn't sure I could suddenly uncork that kind of emotion. How could I access tears on demand when I didn't even know how to muster them for myself? I had a lot of anxiety about whether I'd be able to do it, the kind of anxiety that tells you: I *need* to conquer this.

That was the gem that film gave me—it pushed me to figure out how to access my emotions, particularly my pain. I worked with an acting coach named Harold Guskin, who started by talking to me about breathing, and how we use breath to control our feelings. He walked me through an exercise that mimicked what we tend to do naturally when we start to feel emotional—which is, basically, to hold our breath. The goal of the exercise was to help me understand how to take whatever emotion was in the scene and connect it with my physical being. As I was sitting there with him, I became aware of how much I held my breath. A quick breath out, then in, and hold it: I'd been doing that for years whenever I was pricked by fear or sorrow or rage. I'd shut down my emotions by using my breath to literally keep my feelings inside.

That information alone was liberating. That flash of awareness was so simple and yet so revelatory, knowing that those emotions were *there*, in me, that I wasn't missing a chip. Because of *Ghost*, I learned how to breathe, and that helped me begin to unlock my feelings, to connect to them in a healthier way. It had a huge impact on me, and how I looked at myself. There were definitely some blocks (and there still are), but it was one of those great moments that not only opened things up for me personally but also was very powerful in the film. I was amused, recently, when I was at Sundance promoting the movie *Corporate Animals*, and a young journalist told me his favorite moment from any movie was when a single tear rolled down my cheek in *Charlie's Angels: Full Throttle* as I said, "I was never good: I was great." Then he mentioned *Ghost*, and asked, "How does it feel to be the most iconic crier in cinema history?" That tickled me: to think I went from not crying *ever* to being known for my weeping.

One of the things that connected people to my performance in *Ghost*, I think, was the level of vulnerability that I managed to reveal—and actually feel. My whole experience making that film was great, not least because we shot in L.A., so there was no conflict with Bruce about me being away. And there was good chemistry between the cast and crew. Sometimes on a set, you feel like nothing's working and you're just struggling to get through every scene. But *Ghost* was the kind of set where there was just an overall ease of alignment and you could feel it all coming together. Not too long ago I was interviewed for a documentary about Patrick. They showed me some behind-the-scenes footage I'd never seen before, and I was struck by the comfortable, open sweetness between us. That's just who he was.

At the first screening of the movie, everybody from my agents to the studio executives were ecstatic—and so was I. I took their experienced assessments to heart: if they felt it was going to do great, then I did, too. We were all so excited to read the reviews, but when the first one appeared, it was horrible. The reviewer just hated *Ghost*, which marked a turning point for me: better not to read reviews, I decided, because if you attribute weight and power to the good, then you have to do it for the bad, too, and you're always going to be at someone else's mercy.

Meanwhile, the movie was a smash hit at the box office when it opened in the summer of 1990: it brought in over $200 million. And it had a lasting impact. To this day, I hear from people all over the world about what a profound effect that film had on them, particularly people who have lost someone, and felt the movie had given them hope.

Ghost was also my first "grown-up" movie. By that I mean I was included in every aspect of the creative process, from the production design to the music. We would look at the dailies at lunch every day, and there was a clear sense of thoroughness and total professionalism about the whole endeavor. There was some of that on *About Last Night*, of course—maybe *Ghost* felt different for me because I was a little bit older and less insecure. But I also think it had a certain magic, and audiences could feel that on a visceral level.

The naysayers were proven wrong about *Ghost* when it was nominated for five Academy Awards. I was delighted when Bruce Joel Rubin won the Oscar for Best Original Screenplay, and Whoopi got hers for Best Supporting Actress. I did okay myself, earning a Golden Globe nomination for Best Actress; Julia Roberts won for *Pretty Woman*, another movie that has stood the test of time. Today, if you happen upon either *Ghost* or *Pretty Woman* on cable, they may seem like period pieces. But chances are you will find it surprisingly difficult to change the channel, nonetheless. Because both of those films, dated though they may be, have the most important thing in a feel-good movie: heart.

MY PROFESSIONAL LIFE was soaring. My personal life was painful. Right before Rumer's second birthday, Bruce was getting ready to go do a film that was shooting in Europe, *Hudson Hawk*. There was a lot of buzz around it: it had a huge budget; Bruce had worked on the story and cowritten some of the songs, and he had a lot riding on the film. Just before he left, he dropped a bombshell: "I don't know if I want to be married."

I felt like I had been sucker punched. "Well, you *are* married, and you have a kid," I pointed out. "So what do you want to do?"

Bruce and I had met, married, had a baby, and just done a *lot*, very quickly—it was as if he woke up a few years later and thought, *Whoa, is this what I want? Or do I really want to be free?* I think that as a true Pisces, he was struggling to resolve a conflict within himself: he wanted family and grounding, but he also craved excitement and novelty. Basically, he wanted to do whatever the fuck he wanted. Not so unusual in men that age—he was thirty-six at the time—and throw in celebrity and money? You do the math.

The strong, tough part of me thought, *If this isn't 100 percent what you want, then you* should *get out. I need a husband who I don't have to convince to be in this marriage.* But Bruce didn't want to be the guy who walked out on his family, who did that to his kid. Even though I was terrified and finding it difficult to wrap my head around the enormity of what was happening, I kept saying over and over, "Then go." But he couldn't quite commit to *that* any more than he could fully commit to me. When he left to do *Hudson Hawk*, things were in a very precarious state. I went over to visit once, and, frankly, I had the feeling that he had screwed around. It was tense and it was weird and there was just stuff that didn't seem kosher.

I was wrestling with a sense of rejection and uncertainty

I just couldn't shake when I was offered a movie called *The Butcher's Wife*. I shouldn't have done that film, but for reasons that had nothing to do with Bruce. My agent at the time talked me into doing *The Butcher's Wife* for the money, to get my price up. I've never done a movie just for money again. It was never how I'd worked, and it was a disaster of an experience that I didn't want to repeat. I didn't feel confident going into it, I didn't feel confident while I was there, and I didn't trust the director. The movie rested on me, but I didn't have half the experience of the other actors, Jeff Daniels, Frances McDormand, and Mary Steenburgen. I was intimidated, and I didn't have the confidence to ask them for help. Instead, I assumed that everyone was judging me to be a fraud, and that I was letting them down. I had to employ a southern accent, and I worried I sounded ridiculous.

I played a clairvoyant woman who visualizes her future husband—a butcher from New York—and to help us all understand psychics better, the producers brought one on the set. The very first thing she said to me during our session was, "Your daughter's really beckoning for you to have another child." She wasn't wrong: Rumer had been clamoring for a sibling; she was dying for a baby brother.

It was hard to imagine that happening right then. Bruce was in Europe shooting, and he was furious with me for going back to work, on top of all the mixed feelings he already had about our marriage. We had made a pact never to be apart from each other for more than two weeks, and then to spend at least four days together, but I had made that impossible by doing this film. I had a very rebellious reaction to Bruce in general. I just didn't buy the "You're the king" kind of thing, which he thrived on. Plus, telling me "I don't know if I want to be married" is not exactly the way to *my* heart.

But when he got back, the very first time we had sex, I got pregnant again. And he was over the moon. Suddenly, it was like we'd never had that conversation about his ambivalence.

CHAPTER 13

In the midst of all this, I was offered the cover of *Vanity Fair*. My publicist and I were ecstatic: I had received a swell of media attention following *Ghost*, but this was the ultimate get for an actress at that time. Annie Leibovitz and I set up a photo session, but the pictures we took didn't work out—I'd had to dye my hair blond for *The Butcher's Wife*, and the editors at *Vanity Fair* said the photographs didn't look like me and they weren't going to use them. We'd have to reshoot.

I was hugely pregnant by the time I was able to do the reshoots with Annie. "If we're shooting me as I am, I want the images to show that I feel sexy and beautiful as a pregnant woman," I told her. It seemed ludicrous to me that, at that time, pregnant women were invariably portrayed as sexless. Women hid their pregnancies under tentlike clothes instead of flaunting their new curves the way you often see today. There may have been celebration at the news of a woman's pregnancy, and a celebration at the birth of the baby, of course, but when you looked at pop culture, it was like there was nothing in between. I wanted to change that and do something that glamorized pregnancy instead of playing it down, and that was very much the tone of what Annie and I set out to accomplish with the photographs. They were wonderfully sensual, provocative photos of me all done up—hair, makeup, jewelry—as if it were a fashion shoot that just happened to feature an enormously pregnant model. In one image I wore a green satin robe that fell open to expose my stomach; in another I was in a black bra and high heels holding my swollen belly.

The very pregnant, very nude picture of me on the August 1991 cover of *Vanity Fair* was actually one Annie thought she was taking just to give as a present to Bruce and me. It was understated, soulful, without the glitz of the photos we assumed the magazine would want. Annie shot it at the very end, when we were already "finished," or so we thought at the time. In what became an iconic image, I had one arm draped across my breasts, the other cupping my belly, and that's it. I remember saying to her, "It would be amazing if they had the courage to use *this* for the cover." And, amazingly, they did.

SOMETHING ELSE MOMENTOUS happened during that pregnancy. My agent called to say I was a "person of interest" for a part in *A Few Good Men*, which would star Jack Nicholson and Tom Cruise. "But you'll have to audition for it," he told me. "Would you be willing to do that?" We both knew that the director, Rob Reiner, could have simply cast me without an audition: I had done enough work at that point for him to see what I was like on-screen, and I had reached a certain level of success—once you've been in some big movies, you don't usually get asked to audition. At the same time, I'd never had a problem with having to *earn* a part: it helped quiet the insecure voice in my head asking, *Is it okay that I'm here?*

I was seven months pregnant—enormous—when I waddled in to read with Tom Cruise for the part of Lieutenant Commander JoAnne Galloway in front of Rob Reiner. I was nervous: Rob Reiner was a very well-respected director; Aaron Sorkin had written a great script; and I thought the world of Jack Nicholson and Tom—whom I'd read with four years earlier for the part of his love interest in *Top Gun*. I'd botched that screen test out of nerves, and the part went to Kelly McGillis. I was determined to do better this time, and I must have, because soon after that audition they offered me the part.

The first thing in my head was, *I'm going to have to get in shape really fast.* On paper, it worked: The baby was due in August. Rehearsals for *A Few Good Men* were to start in September. It would be tight, but I'd have a month to get myself back into movie shape after the baby was born.

I knew I needed to get—and stay—fit, even while I was pregnant, for this to work, so I hired a trainer. He actually ended up moving his family into our guesthouse in Idaho; he had a little boy around Rumer's age, and they spent all summer playing together. My thirteen-year-old nephew Nathan, George and DeAnna's oldest son, came, too, along with Morgan, who was carving out a career for himself in special effects, after completing his tour as a Marine in Desert Storm. We had some really nice time as a family that July, and I worked out with my trainer every day. First it was walks, then the walks turned into hikes. We started biking together in the mountains, and I must have been a sight, pumping away with my knees completely splayed out to make room for my belly.

We were at a Carole King charity concert the night my water broke, almost a month before the baby was due. It was only a partial break—enough to make a puddle around my feet. Everyone around me panicked, but the hospital was a short hop away and the doctor there turned out to be just as wonderful as the one who'd delivered Rumer in Kentucky. He had done a lot of volunteer work in South America and Africa and had dealt with plenty of emergency situations, enough to know that this wasn't one. "I think you're fine," he said. "You should go on home." Very few doctors would have allowed that because they would have been afraid of infection, but he was calm and told me, "Just watch out for a temperature and don't take a bath."

I didn't go into full labor for two more days, and even then, the contractions were intermittent. I went to the hospital when they became steady, and the whole household came with me: Bruce, my nephew, my brother, Rumer, a babysitter, plus a friend of ours from Hailey. While I tried to kick-start things by pedaling away on the stationary bike in the physical therapy room, my cheering section was setting up camp, ordering pizza, and playing board games. The doctor finally said he didn't think my water was going to break on its own—it hadn't with Rumer, either—and at the very instant he broke the water, I went into hard labor.

Scout LaRue Willis was born on the 20th of July 1991, three and a half weeks early. I had read *To Kill a Mockingbird* while I was pregnant, and I named her after its brave young heroine.

VANITY FAIR HIT the stands soon after Scout was born, and it set off a firestorm. I was shocked, though the magazine's editor, Tina Brown, evidently was not: anticipating the controversy the cover story would ignite, she had tucked the magazine in a white sleeve, which concealed my pregnant body from the neck down. Only my face showed, along with the cover line "More Demi Moore."

Even with the sleeve, some newsstands refused to carry the magazine. People went *insane* about it. One camp called it disgusting pornography and accused me of exhibitionism. Another saw it as a liberating breakthrough for women. All *I* had meant to accomplish was to show that a pregnant woman could be beautiful and glamorous—that there didn't have to be a disconnect between "sexy" and "mother," especially when you consider that sex is what makes you a mother in the first place! I didn't think I was making a political statement, I just thought I was portraying pregnancy the way I experienced it: as something lovely, natural, and empowering.

I received a lot of letters from women, many of whom identified themselves as feminists, thanking me for taking pregnancy out of the closet and showing it as a glorious part of being female. It's hard to believe now when every celebrity proudly gets her picture taken with her "baby bump," but at that point it really seemed revolutionary to a lot of people, and the reaction was overwhelming, both pro and con. To this day, I am probably more closely identified with that photograph than with any movie I've ever made. I'm very proud of it, truthfully, because it's something I've done that really moved the needle culturally, whether I intended it to or not. The American Society of Magazine Editors voted it the second-best cover in half a century, the top spot going to another one of Annie's photographs, picturing a nude John Lennon snuggling up to a fully clothed Yoko Ono and taken just five hours before Lennon was shot.

In 2011, on the twentieth anniversary of my pregnant cover, the art director George Lois, who designed all those legendary *Esquire* covers in the sixties—Muhammad Ali as the martyred Saint Sebastian shot full of arrows, Andy Warhol sinking into a tomato vortex in a Campbell's Soup can—posted this on *Vanity Fair*'s website:

A truly great magazine cover surprises, even shocks, and connects in a nanosecond. A glance at the image

by photographer Annie Leibovitz that graced the August
1991 issue of Vanity Fair, *depicting a famous movie star*
beautifully bursting with life and proudly flaunting her
body, was an instant culture buster—and damn the ex-
pected primal screams of those constipated critics, cranky
subscribers, and fidgety newsstand buyers, who the ed-
itors and publishers surely knew would regard a pregnant
female body as "grotesque and obscene." Demi Moore's
hand bra helped to elegantly frame the focal point of this
startlingly dramatic symbol of female empowerment. To
me, quite simply, it was a brave image on the cover of a
great magazine—a stunning work of art that conveyed a
potent message that challenged a repressed society.

To help women love themselves and their natural shapes—
that's a remarkable and gratifying thing to have accomplished,
particularly for someone like me who spent years doing battle
with her body.

IF THE COVER and its repercussions exceeded my dreams,
the article that accompanied it inside the magazine was my
nightmare. The smart and strong cover photo was completely
at odds with the devastating representation of me in that story:
I was portrayed as selfish, egotistical, and pampered. A series
of anonymous quotes claimed that I had gotten *Ghost* because

I'd "married well," and said that "being Mrs. Bruce Willis" had gone to my head—"Swelling it unmercifully." There were complaints about the "entourage factor," assertions that I was "catered to" on the set of *The Butcher's Wife*, where the interview had transpired. I was a prima donna surrounded by sycophants, among whom was listed Rumer's nanny—I was still nursing! *"You try shooting a movie without help while you're breastfeeding!,"* I wanted to scream. Nancy Collins, the journalist who wrote the story, also claimed I "was catered" to by a psychic consultant, when the clairvoyant on set had been brought there by the producers for everyone's benefit, not for me in particular. I told Collins during our interview, "It's a lot more interesting to write about me being a bitch than being a nice woman," regardless of what was actually true. Unfortunately, she proved me right.

Perhaps I overreacted to the negativity in the story. But it did a lot of damage, and became the benchmark on which all subsequent interviews would be based. The distorted portrayal of me as a diva would follow me for years, because anybody doing a story on me or a new movie I was in would first read the *Vanity Fair* piece, and then interview me based on its assertions. The article would also have a subtle negative impact on my career, introducing the myth that I was "difficult."

A lot of ill will would come my way from that one story, but it was also a humbling reality check. If I was somehow conveying a persona that was totally at odds with how I saw myself and who I wanted to be, then something needed to change. And

Grandma Marie and Granddaddy Bill King.

Danny as a young boy; note his lazy eye.

My father, Danny Guynes, far left, with his eight siblings.

My mother, Ginny, as a teenager.

Danny's high school
yearbook photo.

Ginny and Danny at a school dance.

Ginny's high school
yearbook photo.

Ginny's wedding to Charlie Harmon in 1962.

Her wedding to Danny less than a year
later, in February 1963.

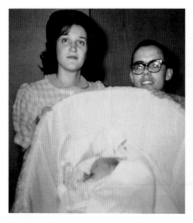

Ginny and Danny with me shortly after my birth; they were only teenagers themselves.

Four generations of women: Great-grandma Metcalf, Ginny (holding newborn me), and Grandma Marie.

With Danny and Grandma Marie. It's impossible to overstate how much my maternal grandmother meant to me, or the stability she provided.

One-year-old me.

Three-year-old me in a treasured photo taken by my dad, and in full cowgirl mode.

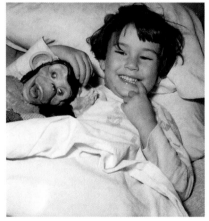

With my beloved monkey. They will always be my favorite.

With Danny just before I was released from my first hospital stay to go home for Christmas.

Fresh out of the hospital and feeding
my new baby brother.

My first pair of glasses.

With Ginny, Morgan, Danny, and
Aunt Betty.

Bath time with Morgan.

My first public performance, playing an ant dancing to "Sugar, Sugar" by
the Archies.

Roommates: my second kidney flare-up, at age eleven, overlapped with Morgan's hernia operation.

With Mom at Christmas, her favorite holiday.

The mascot grows up: cheerleading in Roswell, 1975.

With Dad, Morgan, and my cousins about a year before my parents' divorce.

With Freddy in 1980, a year before we got married.

My uncle George walked me down the aisle at the wedding, which took place four months after Danny's suicide. I was eighteen.

My first "headshot," post–eye surgery.

With DeAnna at the reception. My aunt and uncle were my safe harbor—and they still are today.

On set in Brazil for *Blame It on Rio*, my first big movie break, in 1982.

Happy times with Emilio. Postponing our wedding was one of the hardest things I ever had to do.

With Patsy Rugg in 1996. Patsy was more than my sponsor; she was a surrogate mother.

With Morgan celebrating my twenty-third birthday in New York, where I was making my off-Broadway debut in *The Early Girl*.

Bruce literally swept me off my feet: we met, married, and were pregnant within four months.

Our "second" wedding photo taken by the genius Annie Leibovitz in December 1987 (we had tied the knot in Vegas on November 21st).

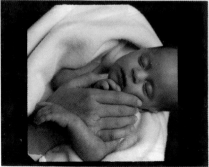

One of the added bonuses of working with Annie was the ability to chronicle the growth of our family over the years.

A decade of work and play, from *Ghost* to *G.I. Jane*. Hunter Reinking (pictured center right) entered our lives about the same time as Tallulah and has been riding this roller coaster with me for over twenty-five years.

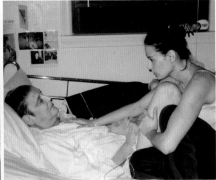

I will be forever grateful for the time I spent caring for my mother in the last months of her life.

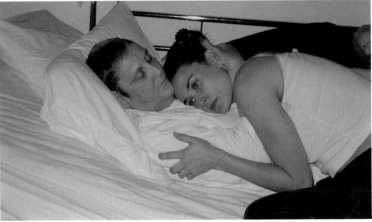

The love and connection Ashton and I shared was magical; while our losses may have been insurmountable, the highs were truly unforgettable. (*Top left photograph by Mario Testino*)

Home is where the heart is: from the top of the mountain with Ariel Levy and Sheri Slater to the ragtag crew at Christmas—Jacqui, Gia, Linda, Masha, Patrick, Rumi Lou, Eric, Greta, Sarah Jane, and Sheri-O. And always, my three little monkeys.

Collins did get one thing right. I remember being struck by this passage:

> *Willis, who has accused the tabloids of trying to break up his marriage, smolders over any suggestion that the relationship is troubled. As for the tabs' ongoing battle to link Willis with other women, Moore is unfazed. "Do I get jealous? Sure. But he doesn't do anything to provoke it, so if I do feel that way, it's something going on in my own head."*
>
> *Does she trust her husband? "Do I trust anybody?" she asks after a long pause. "That's the question. Along the way I've been shown it's O.K. to trust, so I usually go ahead and take the chance. But deep down do I really trust? I don't think so." Moore says she trusts her husband "probably more than I do anybody. But the only person I really trust is my child."*

GINNY MADE MATTERS worse, as she so often managed to. Nude pictures of her began to surface in the tabloids. Her need for attention was so desperate she'd let these rags convince her to pose naked, mimicking the shots I'd done for magazines, including the cover of *Vanity Fair*. It was pitiful. "You're embarrassing yourself!" I told her, but to no avail. In her delusional mind, she believed the people paying her were her friends. I tried to explain to her that these so-called friends were taking advantage of her, but she wouldn't hear me. "You made money modeling," she said. "You just don't want me to."

I'd hit my limit. It probably seems strange, after all the truly ugly things she'd put me through, that Ginny's behavior with the tabloids was what put me over the edge. I think it's because I saw the potential this particular brand of lunacy had to hurt my kids. Honestly, if it had just been me, I probably would have let her continue the cycle of betrayal and disappointment ad infinitum. But there was no way I was going to let her hurt my family.

I broke off all contact with my mother soon after Scout was born. Some of our family members were critical of my choice. But I knew it was the healthiest thing I could do for myself, my girls, and maybe even for Ginny. All the money I'd spent on rehab, the plane tickets I'd bought when she'd called me stranded for some insane reason or other—none of it was actually helping her. It was enabling her. No longer would I hold a futile expectation of her being a mother; no longer would I feel that I bore the responsibility of being *her* mother.

I didn't speak to her again for eight years.

CHAPTER 14

The day after Scout was born, I strapped her into a baby carrier and walked the long loop past the few houses in our neighborhood in Hailey, which is mostly populated by trees and elk. Within a week, I was back to biking, hiking, and working out at the gym five days a week. I nursed Scout as I did Rumer, but where Rumer began to plump up right away, Scout stayed tiny. One day, when she was around five weeks old, a wash of fear came flooding over me that something was really wrong. I rushed her to the doctor, and my concern turned to panic when he weighed her and found she was barely above her birth weight—which had been low to begin with because she had been early.

The doctor stepped out of the examination room and came back with a bottle of formula, and I watched as he nudged the nipple into her mouth and she gulped the liquid down.

The problem with her weight was my fault. The doctor didn't say it in those words, but it was the only conclusion I could reach when he explained that my excessive exercising was creating a surplus of lipase, an enzyme that breaks down fat, in my breast milk. Even though Scout was nursing for hours, she wasn't growing. We would have to add formula to her diet. I was crushed. Nursing for me was such a joyous part of being a mother.

And yet I didn't feel like I could stop exercising. It was my *job* to fit into that unforgiving military uniform I'd be wearing in two months in *A Few Good Men*. Getting in shape for that movie launched the obsession with working out that would consume me over the next five years. I never dared let up.

We went back to L.A., where *A Few Good Men* was filming and Bruce was soon to be shooting *Death Becomes Her* with Goldie Hawn and Meryl Streep. In a stroke of good fortune, both films were being shot on the same lot at a studio in Culver City—which quickly started resembling a day care center. Meryl had just had a baby. I'd just had a baby. Rob Reiner and his wife had a baby. So did the British comedian Tracey Ullman, who was shooting her television show on that lot. We would all wander from one trailer to another with our kids. There's a picture on the wall at my house in Idaho of all the members of what we jokingly called the All-Star Baby Group in that Culver City studio. As it happened, three of those babies—Scout, Jake Reiner, and Tracey Ullman's son, Johnny—grew up to go to the same high school in L.A.

When we started rehearsals for *A Few Good Men*, I managed to fit into that tight uniform, but not without herculean effort. I'd get up early, go for a long run, go to the set, hit the gym, and then feed the baby through the night. It was punishing. I'd gained only twenty-eight pounds with Scout, and I was slowly sloughing it off with my fanatical routine, but one part of my anatomy stayed stubbornly huge: I was alternately nursing Scout and giving her a bottle, so my breasts were painfully full half the time, and I was outrageously busty as a result. (Though often one boob would be much bigger than the other, and the wardrobe people would have to add padding to make them look even.)

I'd always been in awe of Jack Nicholson, and working with him only magnified that feeling. The now-classic payoff line in the movie, which is about two young Marines being court-martialed for murder, comes at the end of what was a long day of shooting the court scene: Jack, playing a Marine colonel, turns on my legal partner, played by Tom Cruise, and snarls, "You can't handle the truth." We had to be on the set all day while they shot the "reverse side," meaning the camera was always on Tom in the courtroom. But Jack delivered that speech all day long, for everybody. You often hear about actors who hold back on their lines when they're not on camera, and save it for their close-ups, but not Jack. I was sitting at the legal table on the set, looking straight at him, and I watched him give 100 percent to his performance all day, to the point where I thought he was going to lose his voice. I was so impressed with that level of generosity: he was giving to his fellow actors at the same level that he gave for the camera when it was on *him*—which is especially hard to keep doing over and over again in a big, emotional scene.

He was not as gracious a few days later, as we waited and waited for him to show up to shoot a scene at a location that doubled for Guantánamo, where the story takes place. The light needed to be in a certain spot for the shot to work, and the sun was getting lower and lower in the sky. Rob Reiner was muttering that it was going to be a disaster and no one could understand why we couldn't just get Jack out of his trailer. Jack appeared at the last moment of light: he is a serious Lakers fan, and he'd been glued to the television set waiting for Magic Johnson to make the announcement that he was HIV positive. Jack knew the announcement was coming, though nobody else did.

What I admired most about *A Few Good Men* was the origin-inality Aaron Sorkin and Rob Reiner showed by not having my character and Tom's get involved in anything romantic, or even unprofessional. There was an expectation at that time on the part of studios and audiences that if an attractive woman showed up on film, it was only a matter of time before you saw her in bed with the leading man, or at least half naked. But Rob and Aaron had the nerve to buck that convention: they thought this story was about something else, and they were right. Years later Aaron told a film school class: "The whole idea of the movie was that these young lawyers were in way over their heads and two Marines were on trial for their lives, so if Tom Cruise and Demi Moore take time out to roll in the hay, I just didn't think we would like them as much for doing that." Sorkin said he wrote to an exec who had been lobbying hard for a sex scene. "I'll never forget what the executive wrote back, which was, 'Well if Tom and Demi aren't going to sleep together why is Demi a woman?' and that completely stumped me."

I loved that my character *didn't* rely on her sex appeal, which was certainly something I hadn't encountered very often in my roles. They presented a woman who was valuable to her colleagues—and to the story itself—because of her compe-tence. The movie was nominated for four Academy Awards and five Golden Globes.

MY HEART SANK as I read the script for my next picture and noted the number of sex scenes I had ahead of me. I wanted to do the movie because it was a great story: a young couple go to Las Vegas in the hope of winning enough money to finance their dream home, which the husband, an architect, wants to build. Instead, they lose all their savings. But the wife, Diana, catches the eye of a billionaire, who makes them an offer: he'll give them a million bucks to spend one night with her. They are conflicted, but they accept, and the story goes on from there.

It was called *Indecent Proposal*, and a great director was making it. Adrian Lyne was known for his moody, sexually charged films—*Fatal Attraction, Flashdance, Jacob's Ladder.* He insisted on every one of his actors auditioning, no matter what. I had actually met with him on almost every film he'd done, including one called *Foxes* when I was still underage— Jodie Foster got the part—but he had never cast me. This time, I made the cut.

Woody Harrelson was going to play my husband. Woody was one of Bruce's best friends, and I knew him really well, too, by that point. That seemed like it could be awkward—kissing him would be like kissing my brother. On the other hand, there was a comfort to working with a friend whom I trusted completely. When Adrian got Robert Redford to play the billionaire, it solidified my feeling that this film would be something unique.

I made a deal with Adrian: he would be free to shoot the sex scenes however he wanted, but in the end I could review the footage and if there was anything I felt was too invasive or gratuitous, he would cut it. It was an arrangement that required a lot of trust on both our parts, and I appreciated his willingness to collaborate like that.

Still, I would be on display again, and all I could think about was my body, my body, my body. I doubled down on my already over-the-top exercise routine. I cut out carbs, I ran and I biked and I worked out on every machine imaginable in the gym we'd installed in the house in Hailey. I was actually feeling comfortable with how I looked when I went in to see Adrian about a month later to talk about costumes. I *finally* had my body where I wanted it.

"You've lost a lot of weight," Adrian said immediately when I walked in for our meeting.

Initially, I took that as a compliment, and I explained that I didn't want to feel self-conscious in all the love scenes coming up, so I'd been working hard on my body. I don't think he listened to a word I was saying. He just kept looking at me with a disturbed expression on his face. Finally, he spat, "I don't want you looking like a fucking man!"

My head was spinning when I left his office. I completely lost it when my agent called later that night and told me, "Adrian is going to fire you if you don't gain at least ten pounds."

We had another meeting, this time with my agent and the head of the studio, as well as Adrian. "You don't know what you're asking me to do," I tried to explain to him. "That's like saying to a heroin addict, 'Go do drugs.'" I did my best to make him understand my struggle, to see how important it was that I not feel self-conscious during the sex scenes, and that I needed to be slim to be comfortable naked on camera. Very reluctantly, Adrian backed down. In fairness, it was his film, and he wanted the leading lady to have a soft, sensuous look, whereas my ideal for myself was to be delicate and svelte like a ballerina. On the one hand, it was my body. On the other, it was his film. There was a little bit of tension and antagonism between us after that—I didn't want him to win, but I knew that a seed had been planted and that it was only a matter of time before my need to please was going to do battle with my desire to be thin. In the very first scene we shot for *Indecent*

Proposal, I was rolling around in my underwear on a bed covered with money.

I knew Glenn Close, and she'd warned me that Adrian was an odd guy to work with on love scenes: she told me he was yelling out encouraging obscenities the whole time she was humping away with Michael Douglas all over that loft in *Fatal Attraction*. Glenn hadn't exaggerated. Adrian is a true voyeur, which is part of why his films are so interesting and potent. But on set it's very kooky: he literally didn't stop talking—practically hollering!—the whole time we were shooting the sex scenes. "Fucking raunchy! Oh God, got a boner on that!" he'd yell. "Come on, grab his dick!" At first it was creepy: here was this guy with this sort of long-haired, British-rocker look, getting all sweaty and worked up, yelling about boners. But once I got used to it, I saw its advantages: having Adrian carry on that way took the focus off my own awkwardness because he was so over the top. Once I knew not to take his outbursts at face value, it was actually pretty hilarious having him yelping on the side-lines while Woody and I tried to simulate lust. And the fact is, when I saw what Adrian had pulled off in the end, I thought it was beautiful. I didn't have to rely on our deal; there was nothing he'd shot that made me uncomfortable, or that seemed prurient or excessive. His movies are erotic, but they aren't sleazy.

The filming was a slog, though. The shooting schedule in Vegas was from four a.m. to four p.m., so every morning I got up at one thirty to start training by two. I ran or biked or worked out in the gym at the Mirage. I finished just in time to jump in the shower and go through hair and makeup. At night, I took care of my little girls, who'd come with me, along with their nanny and my trainer. Then I would get up at one thirty the next morning and do the whole thing all over again.

It caught up with me halfway through the shooting when I felt as if I was coming down with the flu. Adrian wanted to call a sick day, but I said no; I didn't want people talking about how the production had to be stopped because of me—I was still paranoid about being seen as "difficult." Over my objections, Adrian called a doctor to come and see me, and it turned out it wasn't the flu: I had walking pneumonia. This time I had no choice, and neither did Adrian. He had to take an insurance day on my behalf, which is something actors never want to have on their records.

A medical crew came and gave me intravenous antibiotics. I felt better right away, but it was a little scary, so I eased up a bit on my workouts—though not enough for Adrian. The look on his face every time he saw me in sneakers or on a bike was disapproving, bordering on disgusted, and as much as I pushed back, it began to get to me. By the time we finished the movie, he had succeeded in getting inside my head—to the point that I had put on all the weight he had wanted me to gain at the beginning. I was almost unbearably uncomfortable about it. I could see it in the last scenes we shot for the film: I was in this cream dress and my belly was a little "poochy," and I remember

Adrian coming over to me while we were watching the takes and noticing it. I told him, "Do not say one more *word* to me about my body."

As crazy as Adrian and I made each other, I have to say that I've never been shot more beautifully. Everyone looked golden in *Indecent Proposal*, as if we were lit from within. The DP—director of photography—would do the lighting, but then Adrian would come in and rework it himself. His level of focus in terms of lighting and storytelling was incredible: he paid attention to *everything*, down to the details of the costumes. I remember I suggested a black shantung silk dress of my own for the first "date" between my character and Redford's billionaire, and Adrian loved it. He wanted that initial encounter between them to feel elegant, despite the fact that my character had basically turned into a call girl for a night; he wanted to create a situation so romantic, so classy, that it transcended their deal and felt, actually, seductive to the viewer. Adrian even got Herbie Hancock to play piano on the Redford character's yacht while we slow danced in that scene. (I just kept thinking about that iconic moment in *The Way We Were*, when Barbra Streisand takes her gloved hand and brushes Redford's hair out of his eyes. It's not easy being spontaneous with a screen legend, but he couldn't have been more gracious throughout the shoot.) Gone was the raunchy Adrian, and in his place was Adrian the Romantic. He was a perfectionist with a clear vision, and while our ideas about my body clashed rather violently, I don't think he was ever intentionally cruel. He just wanted what he wanted. Good directors always do.

The movie made a whopping $24 million box office in just five days when it opened in April 1993. Though it was universally panned by critics and women's groups—who objected to my character being used as barter—the movie ended up making over $260 million worldwide.

The controversy with feminists was really interesting. The author Susan Faludi accused Robert Redford's character of "raping a woman with money." A critic in the *Los Angeles Times* wrote, "In Hollywood it may be the Year of the Woman, but this year every woman has her price." The *Washington Post* said, "If a man is sold, it's called slavery. In Hollywood, if a woman is sold, it's called romance." I thought that was an oversimplification of a story told with a lot of nuance, which really strikes at the core of our collective fears about marriage. Whether you're a man or a woman, no matter how content you are with someone, there's always that slight anxiety that someone better—richer or prettier or more impressive at whatever it is you are insecure about—will steal your partner's heart away. It was also a movie about the blunt force of money. It asked, For what amount of money would you sell yourself, your spouse, your life?

I never consciously had this thought while we were making the film, but I'm sure simmering away somewhere in my subconscious was the ugliest question I'd ever been asked: "How does it feel to be whored by your mother for five hundred dollars?" *That* was an indecent proposal. Our film, by contrast, was the story of a woman who was precious. A billionaire would give anything for her. Her own husband was nearly destroyed by the thought of losing her, even for a night. She was beloved and respected and had her own career, and, ultimately, she was the one who decided what she wanted, what she would and wouldn't allow to happen to her.

I GOT PREGNANT again. But this time was different. I was throwing up every day. I was in my bed and crawling to the bathroom to vomit and then crawling back. It got to where I couldn't bear to eat because I couldn't bear to throw up anymore. At one point I ended up subsisting on water for seven days.

Bruce and I always tried to do our movies at the same time so we would have our off time together. While I was sick, Bruce occupied the kids—Rumer was five, and Scout was not quite two—taking them for walks in the woods, splashing around with them in the pond in the backyard. He was a great dad, protective and involved, and he was excited we were having another baby. But he was as relieved as I was when the morning sickness passed just in time to pack up the kids and the nannies and the pets—our family circus—and head to Hawaii, where Bruce was scheduled to shoot a film with Rob Reiner called *North*.

Though the timing was a little off—I'd felt like I was just starting to get back into my career groove—I didn't have any second thoughts about having another child. The perfect name for the baby surfaced during an all-girls trip to Fisher Island, off the coast of Miami—the game on that vacation became what to name this new baby. Meg Ryan was there; we had fallen into an easy friendship over the years. I found her open and warm and noncompetitive—a real girl's girl—and we were about the same age, walking the same path. I loved her work, but I loved getting to know her even more. She suggested Tallulah, because both of my other daughters' names had "oo" sounds: Rumer, of course, and Scout's middle name, LaRue. "Tallulah would round out your trio of 'oos,'" Meg said.

I loved the name. Bruce hated it. And the campaign began to convince him. There was the obvious reference to Tallulah Bankhead, which didn't sway him. He warmed up a little when I looked it up in a baby name book and found it derived from the Native American word for "leaping water." And then I pointed out the character Jodie Foster played (at age thirteen) in the musical *Bugsy Malone*. That pushed him over the edge, and he gave in.

Bruce was in New York making *Nobody's Fool* with Paul Newman, and I joined him there with the girls for a visit toward the end of my pregnancy. Scout had come early, so I had lined up doctors in New York just in case, though I was feeling great. But there was a problem, as it turned out. The doctors did an ultrasound and were concerned that the baby seemed awfully small for a February due date. "You can't exercise," they told me. "That has to stop." They wanted to make sure nothing got in the way of her growth. All of a sudden, what had been a standard pregnancy became high risk, and I was afraid to do much more than go to the sink to get a glass of water. I got a little nutty being so confined and stationary. And I grew increasingly concerned because they were scanning me almost every day. All of the baby's vital signs were good, but they couldn't figure out why she wasn't gaining weight.

Back in Hailey after Bruce finished the movie, I immediately consulted my regular OB-GYN. He scanned me and compared the image to the ones I'd brought back from New York. "She really hasn't grown in five days," he told me. "You're full term, and I think you just need to get her out, because there's something going on, and we don't know what it is." He induced labor in our little hospital in Hailey, and Tallulah Belle Bruce Willis entered the world at lightning speed on February 3, 1994—the doctor almost missed the birth because he had gone to change his shoes. She was four pounds, twelve ounces, and looked so much like Bruce I added his name to hers. She was incredibly scrawny—like a little head on a stick—but they gave her oxygen and checked her out, and she was perfectly fine, just underweight.

The truth is, the doctor's wisdom to say, "Let's get her out," probably saved her life. I couldn't be more grateful to him for giving me my third baby girl, my sweet little Lulah.

CHAPTER 15

I would have done anything to take care of my girls. I felt an almost primal need to protect them: I would have taken a bullet for them, robbed a bank—you name it. *That* is what I related to when I read a script based on Carl Hiaasen's book *Strip Tease*. I can't imagine much in this world that would make me more uncomfortable than taking my clothes off and exposing my body and sexuality to an audience of strangers every night, but I would have done it to feed my kids without question, just as the protagonist of that story had. Her name was Erin Grant, and she had worked as a secretary for the FBI before she lost her job and, when she could no longer afford to support her, lost custody of her daughter, too. Erin becomes an exotic dancer because she knows it's a surefire way of earning enough money to get her kid back.

Speaking of money, I was offered a lot of it for that role: over $12 million. No other woman in Hollywood had ever made that much money for a movie. But as it happened, the producers of *Striptease* were in a kind of bidding war with the producers of *G.I. Jane*, another story about a woman who will do whatever it takes to reach her goals, albeit a very different sort of woman with very different goals. (I was actually one of the producers of *G.I. Jane*—I had brought the script to my dream director, the brilliant Ridley Scott, and he said yes, which almost never happens.) I had already signed on to do *G.I. Jane*, so the producers of *Striptease* had to offer more than I'd be paid for *G.I. Jane* in order to go first. And so they did. Suddenly, I was the highest-paid actress in Hollywood.

Bruce was also doing well. He'd been paid over $20 million for the third movie in the *Die Hard* series. Notice the discrepancy. In Hollywood at that time—and, unfortunately, still—for some reason a man is worth almost double what a woman is. But instead of people seeing my big payday as a step in the right direction for women or calling me an inspiration, they came up with something else to call me: Gimme Moore.

Some of it had to do with Bruce and me being so successful as a couple. But nobody gave him a grabby, greedy nickname. He was just a guy doing what guys were supposed to do: earn as much as possible to take care of his family. Women, for some reason, are supposed to earn less—in every job, from the worst to the best—and never push back. That never made sense to me. I didn't go to college. I wasn't raised with money. But I knew enough to know that you want to get paid the most you can for what you do. I had defined myself in opposition to the way my parents supported us through slippery chicanery: I worked hard, and I behaved like a professional. I prided myself on giving my all, not just whatever I could get away with. I had taken part in propelling some big box office hits—my last film, *Disclosure* with Michael Douglas, had been a huge commercial success—and I wanted to be paid accordingly. That's all I was guilty of.

In a funny way, the hate that came at me for choosing to do *Striptease*—and getting paid what I did to star in it—mirrored the disapproval the protagonist, Erin, faced for becoming an erotic dancer. I started going to strip clubs to meet the women working there and hear their stories, and it was a fascinating education. Some of them were dancing to put themselves through school. Some were addicts supporting their habits. There was one really beautiful young single mom who danced all night so she could be with her kids all day—I talked about her when I went on Barbara Walters to promote the film, and said that nobody ought to judge that single mom for working to support her family any more than we'd judge a waitress or a secretary. And I meant it.

I was, again, dubbed an exhibitionist. On one level, I get it, of course: I was dancing around a pole in a G-string. Fair enough. But the ugliness with which people responded to that movie felt tinged with real malice and misogyny.

One of the best things about doing *Striptease* was that I got to spend a lot of time with Rumer, who was seven by then, while I was making it. She begged to be allowed to audition for the role of Erin's daughter, and she nailed it and got the part. I don't deny this had as much to do with me as it did with her considerable on-camera charisma: the director loved the idea of our real-life bond coming through in his film, and he thought she was just adorable (I'm biased, but I think he was right). I had a great time with her, and I was very proud: she was diligent and devoted and a quick study. My critics decreed that I was a bad mother for letting her see me dance topless. I thought that was insane: she'd seen me a lot more than topless many times throughout her young life. Despite all my issues with my body (or maybe *because* of them—I didn't want my girls to inherit my issues), I'd raised them to view nudity as natural and nothing to be ashamed of.

As I said, on a conscious level, what drew me to *Striptease* was the mother-daughter story. But when I think about how unmistakably both that film and *G.I. Jane* required me to focus on and dominate my own body, I am forced to recognize that I was working something out through my choices.

When I was making *Striptease*, for breakfast I would measure out a half cup of oatmeal and prepare it with water, then for the rest of the day I would have only protein and some vegetables— and that was it. And the crazy thing is, even eating like that, even working out six days a week, it was not like I was rail thin. I am convinced that it was a kind of mental and emotional holding on. I was gripping so tight in every way—to my marriage, to my career, to my exercise and diet routines—that my body wouldn't let go of anything. The only place I felt truly comfortable with myself was as a mom, a role that to me was at the heart of that film.

If all this obsessing about my body sounds crazy to you, you're not wrong: eating disorders *are* crazy, they are a sickness. But that doesn't make them less real. When you are afflicted with a disease, you can't just decide not to have it, no matter how miserable it's making you.

I THINK VERY few people who aren't athletes or members of the military themselves can truly grasp what I went through to transform myself to star in *G.I. Jane*. It is the film I am most proud of, because it was the hardest for me to make— emotionally, physically, and mentally—and I had to commit to the part as much as I imagined my character, Lieutenant Jordan O'Neil, was committed to becoming the first female Navy SEAL.

I was completely taken with the story: Lt. O'Neil is set up by a female U.S. senator to be the first woman to go through Navy SEAL training, but she has no idea that the senator is using her as a bargaining chip—and fully expects her to fail. O'Neil is beaten up, ridiculed, and nearly drowned, but against all odds she succeeds. That grit, that absolute refusal to go down, despite everything she's up against, spoke to me.

It was also a timely subject: the issue of women in combat was a hot topic following the Gulf War. By law, women were not allowed in combat, but in contemporary warfare, there was really no such thing as a front line. Women weren't safe anywhere in war, but neither did they have the same opportunities as men to advance in their respective services. The Navy and the Air Force went "coed" in 1993, but the Army and Marine Corps held firm on the combat exclusion for women, as did elite units like the Navy SEALs, maintaining that women could simply never be as strong as men.

Getting in shape for the Navy's most punishing physical trial gave a new definition to the word *extreme*. If I was going to be realistic in the part, I knew I had to go through whatever physical challenges Lt. O'Neil would. They put us through a two-week modified SEAL training, and it was just forty guys and me. On the first morning, I woke up at five a.m., took a handful of vitamins, and then they had us run a timed mile. I promptly threw up. By the end of the day, I had horrendous blisters from my boots and could barely walk. One of our SEAL consultants on the film, Harry Humphries, took me aside and said quietly, "Listen, you don't have to do all of this." I thought, *I'm playing an officer. A leader. If I stop now, I'll never get anyone's respect.* I told Harry just to get me some tape for my feet.

It was hard-core. Sam Rockwell was on that film initially, but he didn't make it through the training—he told Carson Daly years later that he was afraid he was going to get sick filming the scuba scenes at night in the frigid water.

On my second day, I was a few minutes late to the training session. The guys were already in formation, and I tried to sneak in at the back of the line unnoticed. "Jordan! Front and center," screamed one of our SEAL team commanders. (They never called me by my real name when we were training.) I ran up in front of him, and as I stood there he yelled, "Who the fuck do you think you are? Drop your fucking ass down." Which means lean and rest: get in a push-up position and hold it. And everyone else was forced to do the same. By the end of that training, though, I was tougher than most of the guys. He'd yell at them, "Are you gonna let yourself get beat by some mother of three?"

The only strength difference between the guys and me by the end was that I could never, ever, get past three pull-ups—four tops. That was the bane of my training existence. No matter how ripped I got, I actually had to cheat on-screen with those. I did my two or three and sometimes I even needed a little help to really nail those.

I finagled a meeting with a high-ranking admiral in Coronado as part of my research, and he confirmed that the only physical difference between men and women candidates for the Navy SEALs would come down to upper-body strength. "Other than that," he told me, "it's purely mental." Our conversation gave me a defining clarity on what I needed to bring to the character of Lt. O'Neil. I could portray her physical strength, but in the end, what was even more important was having the mental resilience to stick with it, no matter what.

I needed that fortitude when we started filming. It was physically and mentally grueling, especially the scene in which O'Neil is one of the SEAL candidates "captured" by a simulated enemy, and, as prisoners of war, they learn SERE, which stands for Survival, Evasion, Resistance, Escape. In the Resistance segment, the captives are tortured to extract information, and I had to engage in a brutal fight with the master chief, played brilliantly by Viggo Mortensen, who in addition to pretending to be an enemy has always been anti-woman, and is trying to show the male candidates what a liability and a danger a female would be on the battlefield. He forced my head underwater and kept it down almost as long as I could hold my breath, then let me come up for a gulp of air before slamming my head back under. It was so realistic, one of the assistant directors was worried I'd drown. Honestly, there were moments when I was afraid of that myself.

RECENTLY, I CAME across a column the beloved movie critic Roger Ebert wrote after an advance screening of *G.I. Jane*. It was, he observed, "intriguing to watch her work with the image of her body. The famous pregnant photos on the cover of *Vanity Fair* can be placed beside her stripper in *Striptease*, her executive in *Disclosure* and the woman in *Indecent Proposal* who has to decide what a million dollars might purchase; all of these women, and now O'Neil, test the tension between a woman's body and a woman's ambition and will. *G.I. Jane* does it most obviously, and effectively." It was gratifying to see that someone as smart as Ebert got it.

Unfortunately, his thoughtful take on the film was an outlier. Even before the movie came out, people who hadn't seen it were already slamming it. It felt like a kind of collective decision just to trash me and treat me as the joke I'd always feared I was.

This was really hard because *G.I. Jane* was a true labor of love, a role that I believed in completely. I was emotionally invested in the story, the message, and the provocative questions it raised. And I thought it was, in fact, a really good film.

Granted, this was the first movie portraying women in combat—or one woman, anyway—and it certainly was pushing the envelope by showing the raw physical dynamic involved and asking the question, If you've got the skill, why shouldn't it be an option? The one-two punch of me being paid more than any woman to date—and equal to many men in my industry—and then playing a woman who was just as strong as a man was just too much for a lot of people.

All the criticism of *G.I. Jane* and *Striptease* was a lot to absorb. The takeaway seemed to be that I had betrayed women in *Striptease* and betrayed men in *G.I. Jane* and gotten paid a lot to do it—and that nobody could forgive me for that. I absorbed all that negativity without really working through it.

Bruce was working the whole time I was, and we were disconnected from each other emotionally. Our life was all about logistics surrounding the kids. And while Bruce was always proud of me doing well, I don't know that he was always comfortable with the attention that came with it.

It didn't occur to me to talk with someone about how I was struggling—in truth, it didn't even occur to me that I was *allowed* to struggle. That it was okay for me to have a problem. I just had to figure this shit out on my own.

I HAD BULKED up enormously making *G.I. Jane*, and I weighed 138 pounds by the time it wrapped. (I don't think it was Bruce's favorite look.) My neck was huge. My back was huge. When I finished the movie, there were pants that I could no longer pull up over my thigh muscles. It was heady being that strong and powerful, but it was not a look I intended to stick with, any more than my shaved head.

My usual reaction would have been to start starving myself again, to begin an exercise regime designed to reduce the bulk, but I did neither. I had reached my limit. When I got home to Idaho, I had an epiphany in the shower one day: *I just want to be my natural size*. I didn't want to starve myself anymore. I didn't want to assess my success as a human being based on how skinny I could get. I was curious: What would my natural size *be* with no manipulation? And I was finally willing to accept whatever the answer might be. I could barely remember a time when I wasn't trying to dominate and control my body—for a long time, it was the only thing I could control. I had a realization that holding on to this weight was a way to protect myself. I added into my daily prayer a new mantra: to have the courage to be seen without padding or protection. I couldn't go on fighting my body and my weight; I had to make peace.

I started by giving up hard exercise. I never went back into the gym in the house. Never. I had spent six painful years in there, starting with Scout's birth in 1991 and finishing after *G.I. Jane* in 1997, and I was burned out. I literally couldn't look at a gym. The room it occupied is now my office.

At the same time, I changed my whole way of dealing with food. Rather than look at it as something to conquer, I decided to try eating when I was hungry and stopping when I was full. I made new rules that didn't include observing breakfast, lunch, and dinner. I just ate when I was hungry, and if that meant I didn't want to eat until lunch, I didn't have to. Over the course of all the different diets I had been on, I had come to realize what worked for me and what didn't. I knew that I needed more protein than carbs; I knew that if I ate a little bit at a time, I digested better. I would still sit down with the children when they had their meals, but I wouldn't necessarily eat just because of the time of day. I no longer had lunch or dinner business meetings. I'd only plan a meal with people I knew well enough to relax with.

The weight came off. It was most apparent in the spring of 1997 when we were starting to prepare for the Cannes Film Festival. Elizabeth Taylor was recovering from brain surgery; she asked me to host her Cinema Against AIDS event in Cannes, and I happily accepted. Bruce's film *The Fifth Element* was opening the festival. I was getting the clothes organized for the many days of events, and we picked them out and then did fittings. Without dieting or doing any kind of extreme exercise, I had lost about thirty pounds in just over three months.

I had finally reached a truce with my body. I would need that peace to get through what came next.

I HAD JUST returned from the press tour for *G.I. Jane* when I got a call from DeAnna: my mother was dying. She had metastatic lung cancer and had recently been diagnosed with a brain tumor on top of that.

If I wanted to reach any kind of understanding with her in this lifetime, it was now or never.

PART III
SURRENDER

CHAPTER 16

At first, I thought it was a scam. I imagined showing up at the hospital, only to find that my mother was fine and had gotten paid to deliver me to the paparazzi. I didn't tell her I was coming, and when I arrived in Farmington, New Mexico, there were no cameras. Instead, there was my mom, staying at my aunt Carolyn's house in a hospital bed she'd had installed in her own bedroom. Ginny was missing all of her hair from chemo, except for one resilient little red tuft. She was gravely ill.

During the eight years we'd been out of touch, Ginny had remarried not once but three times. One of the men had been so abusive she had to be hospitalized after the worst of his beatings. Morgan thought she kept getting married so she could change her name and clean up her credit rating. To this day, DeAnna believes that she and my father never actually divorced, and that all of her subsequent marriages were illegal. One thing seems to be certain: after my dad's death, no matter who she was married to, Ginny always kept a picture of Danny on her nightstand.

I think that in a messed-up way, my mother's relationship with my dad had anchored her. I'm not saying it was healthy, but the constant competition to see who could hurt the other one more, who had the most power at any given moment, had channeled a lot of her energy in a specific direction. Without him, she was completely lost and increasingly at the mercy of her addiction and her bipolarity, which had finally been diagnosed. And now her body was giving out.

When she was hurting me, I couldn't really see past that. I felt unsafe and betrayed and, on the deepest level, devastated that she didn't love me enough to be a better mother. To not exploit me for money. To behave herself at my wedding. To pick me up from school when she said she would. To protect me from Val. And all the rest of it. I have since come to understand that there is no such thing as someone "loving you enough" to be better. People can only be as good as they are, no matter how much they love you.

That's the bad news. The good news is that you have the power to hold their actions differently in your own mind and heart. You can choose to believe that your value is inherent, it's yours, and that the way your mother treated you says something about her, not you. Or you can choose to believe that your mother's neglect means that you are unlovable and worthless. As long as you keep that wound from closing, you'll be sore.

When I decided to care for my mother at the end of her life, I began to heal the wound.

THE FIRST TIME I made the trip to Farmington, DeAnna and Morgan came with me to see Ginny at Carolyn's house, and we were there for a short time. The second time, I got a call that Ginny might not make it through the night, and I rushed back to New Mexico with Bruce and the girls. My mother hadn't seen Rumer since she was a two-year-old toddler; now she was ten. Scout, who was seven, and Lulah, who was four, she'd never met. I think the influx of all these people and so much energy buoyed her, and between that and the steroids the doctor put her on, she managed to stay alive for another three and a half months.

I stayed for the duration. I lived at my aunt's. Bruce— who really stepped up and was truly supportive during that period—went back to Idaho with the kids, who had school, and returned with them to visit me many times during the next few months. It was beautiful having the company of my daughters, who were at the beginning of their lives, when I was spending so much time with my mother, who was at the end of hers.

Hunter Reinking, who'd been my assistant since the movie *Now and Then*, joined me in New Mexico to help out. He took the night shifts with me; we would doze during the day when Aunt Carolyn took over. I still had some of my *G.I. Jane* muscles, so I was strong enough to lift Ginny into the tub for her baths. My mom was so weak she couldn't hoist her ever-present Diet Coke, or raise the cigarettes she never gave up, to her lips. There was no reason to deny her the pleasure of smoking at that point: the damage was already done. So I would light her cigarettes and hold them to her mouth while she puffed away. She would take an orgasmic drag and sigh, "Ooh, that was good for me." I don't know if it was an act of solidarity or just a way of handling the stress, but I started smoking again myself.

One of the things that had always frustrated me about my mom was her insistence on her own victimhood. When she was dying, for once she really *was* the victim. In a way, I think that made it easier for her to be her. It certainly made it easier for me to forgive her, to have compassion for her, and to give her the kind of love and attention she'd always craved. She finally got what she'd wanted her whole life: to be taken care of. To be looked after. And really, in our own way, isn't that what we all want?

I'm sorry that she didn't get the chance to learn that a feeling of security can come from the inside, from yourself. I know that she never was able to overcome the feeling of being unloved and that she carried the trauma of rejection and blame until the very end. I grasped while I was taking care of her a real sense of the innocence of her soul. And I was able to see that she came into this world like we all do: wanting to find happiness, wanting to feel loved, wanting to feel like she belonged. She didn't start life with a plan to be hurtful and neglectful. She just didn't have the tools to navigate out of her own pain. When I consider now how young she was when she had me, I think: *My God, she was just a kid.* My daughters are older now than Ginny was when she had me—much. And they're just finding out who they are.

Ginny sounded very much like a kid at the end, lapsing into delusions of being a six-year-old, insisting that she wanted a bicycle for Christmas. Other times she was an adult but didn't know her father had died, and she talked a lot about his taking her "to the party." When she was clearheaded, sometimes I'd try to talk about real things that I hoped to get some closure on. There was still the little-girl part of me who wanted answers. Ginny was never truly able to hear it, or take responsibility. The most that she could give in acknowledgment was to say, "I wish it could have been different." Which, in a way, was a lot. It was a hell of a lot more than nothing. Because it told me she knew that it wasn't okay. That things that had happened to me were wrong.

I started thinking about the good in her. She was so creative. She was resourceful. She could be very loving and generous, always taking people in. She had so much more to her than just what she was able to live out in her fifty-four years. She died on July 2, 1998.

Bruce was there with the kids, so we had all stayed at a hotel the previous night. When the phone rang at six a.m., I sat up in bed, knowing what I was about to be told. "Please hold the phone up to her ear," I asked Aunt Carolyn. I whispered what

I needed to tell my mother into the phone: "I love you." I did. I still do.

Then I drove back to Carolyn's house, where Ginny had stopped breathing in her hospital bed, and I took a few minutes alone with her, holding her hand. I didn't cry then, and I didn't cry when I went into the little bathroom off her room and closed the door. I had a rush of clarity as I stood absolutely still. All of the emotions that I felt toward Ginny—my anger, my pain, my hurt—were *mine*. The vessel for them was gone now. Whatever *her* issues were, and God knows there were plenty, she'd taken them with her. It was a liberating moment. I was flooded with compassion for the pain she had held all her life and had no way to work through or overcome. I felt sad for this wounded child who had never developed beyond the emotional level of a teenager. That understanding freed me to start to be more forgiving toward myself, and to quit working so hard not to be my mother.

I was only in the bathroom for three or four minutes, but when I opened the door, I felt very calm about entering whatever the next phase of my life would be. I had shed such a heavy load, I felt almost light-headed.

IT IS NOT unusual, from what I hear, to go from feeling like your spouse's lover and best friend to feeling, over time, like he is just someone with whom you negotiate logistics. That's basically what happened with Bruce and me. Only we barely had time to be a couple before we became parents. We had a whirlwind, truncated infatuation that morphed into a full-on family all in our very first year. When reality set in, I don't know if we really knew each other. Soon it was just a life of coordinating details, trying to sync our schedules.

In some ways, I think our marriage was prolonged by our frequent, extended separations. In the first two years of Tallulah's life, I was in eight films, and so was Bruce. My production company, Moving Pictures, was in full swing. And we had three little girls under the age of ten, who were our first priority. It's not surprising we barely had time for each other.

With each of us going full tilt on our careers, we had a perfect kind of distraction for our energy. When we were together, we had the kids in common, and we focused on them. Bruce was tormented, I think, by his ambivalence about being married throughout our time together—at least that's where *I* felt he was during our entire marriage. I felt pain for him and frustration for me and then, eventually, deep hurt. We're all longing to be wanted, to be reassured, and he couldn't give me that because he really didn't *know* what he wanted. Honestly, I think both of us from the outset were more passionate about having kids than we were about being married, and in the end, the kids were—and always will be—what we have together.

Of course, his ambivalence wasn't our only problem. There were elements of Bruce's personality that were similar to my mother's: they were both unpredictable and sometimes impulsive, and that made me feel unsure of my footing. I never knew what mood he'd be in or whether his feelings for me would have changed since the day before. I was used to this from growing up with Ginny, and I recycled my coping mechanism on Bruce, by becoming completely self-sufficient. Same dance, different partner.

I always maintained a kind of emotional buffer, like a moat around a castle, so that I wouldn't be dependent on him or get too wounded when he shifted from hot to cold. It never occurred to me that strength and independence could be a weakness until the day Bruce came into my office, the retired gym in Hailey, and told me, "You know, I feel like if I wasn't here, you could just go on without skipping a beat."

He's right, I thought. The defensive armor I'd become accustomed to wearing was so ironclad, there was no room inside it for someone else. And I realized—too late—that this was a limitation as well as a protection. I recognized how my inability to express need was cheating him out of the chance to fulfill mine. By maintaining my childhood resolve not to be a burden on anyone, what I was really doing was avoiding exposing any vulnerability. When he would ask, "Do you mind if I go do this?"—an overnight trip with the boys to Vegas, for instance, or another gig with his band—and I'd *always* say, without a moment's hesitation, "Go ahead—we'll be fine," part of him was glad he'd married someone so accommodating. But part of him was hearing, on the deepest level, that his presence didn't matter. That I didn't need him.

So Bruce and I were trapped in our dance. He felt locked out by my self-reliance, which hurt him in ways he couldn't face and fed his ambivalence about our marriage. My response to his uncertainty was hurt of my own that *I* couldn't face, which fed my self-protective independence. And on and on, toward infinity.

While I was caring for my mom, Bruce and I decided to separate. We made the decision together while he was with me in New Mexico, visiting with the girls. We wanted to wait to announce it publicly until after my mother passed, so that her funeral would be focused solely on her, as it ought to be, and there wouldn't be the distraction of the media onslaught that would inevitably follow any word of our split. We knew the tabloids would be all over us no matter how the information came out, but we figured that releasing the story ourselves, together, when we were ready as a family, would create a different kind of energy.

Unfortunately, that's not the way it happened. We got a call from our lawyer within days of our decision, saying he'd learned that the tabloids had—somehow—been tipped off, and they would be running a story about our breakup the very next day. It felt awful, as it always does when you learn that someone you trust (Because who else would know? We had hardly told a soul!) is quite literally selling you out. Usually, whatever the story is that the tabloids have gotten ahold of is a little bit right and a *lot* wrong, but that little bit that's true is just enough to make you feel totally exposed, especially when they claim that their source is "someone close to you." That "someone" could be as removed as a guy who overheard someone you know talking at a restaurant, or it could be a person you think is a dear friend who is getting paid to reveal your secrets. It makes you question the loyalty of everyone around you and leaves you with a terrible feeling in the pit of your stomach. Anyway, I had a pit in my stomach, a dying mom, and a marriage that was ending when we got that call from our lawyer. We didn't want to give the tabloids the satisfaction of breaking the story, so we announced our split that day ourselves. (Gratifyingly, our preemptive strike did achieve the desired effect. "The couple confirmed the breakup late Wednesday in a brief press release that was disappointingly [for Enquiring minds] bereft of details," a journalist wrote at the time on E! News. "The hand-out said Bruce and Demi were 'ending' their union. And that was about it.")

We would have preferred to have had more time to deal with our own feelings and to sit down with our children to tell them in the most loving, supportive way possible what was going to happen. Instead, we were rushed and upset. You want to be able to work through a situation like this (or, really, any situation) from the inside out, not the outside in, but we didn't get that chance. We made what we thought was the best decision for all of us, and luckily the children were so young when we told them about our separation that they couldn't really comprehend what it meant. It was hardest for Rumer, of course, who was ten and had the clearest sense of what was about to change—of what we were all losing.

CHAPTER 17

Recently, I did an on-camera interview with a young man who was a total film buff, and he told me how much he loved *G.I. Jane*, how he'd watched it recently and felt it really held up. Then he said, "They were *so* rough on you in the press back then—and it was a great film! What was that about?" I told him, "You have no idea how nice it is to hear that you could see that was going on." *G.I. Jane* never got its due, in my opinion—quite the contrary. Between its savage reception, and Bruce and me splitting up, *and* my mom dying, I was totally wrung out by the end of 1998.

Unfortunately, I had already contracted to do a movie in France called *Passion of Mind* well before Bruce and I made our announcement, and before I knew my mother was dying. I was miserable in Paris. I'd taken the girls along and put them in school there for the four months we needed to be in France, but to get to the movie location on time, I had to leave our rented house at five thirty a.m., before they were awake. By the time I returned, they'd always gone to bed. There was almost no point in their being with me. This was no way for us to live at a moment when there was this huge change taking place in our family, the biggest upheaval so far in my children's lives. They needed more of me than this, and, frankly, I needed more of them. I made a decision: no more movies; no more running around. I wanted to be at home in Hailey with my girls. If I couldn't give them a mother and father who were married, I wanted them at least to have a stable home and a consistent routine. For the next five years, I became something I'd never been before: a full-time mom.

Bruce and I did everything we could think of to make the split as easy as possible for our children, but of course there were challenges. Scout, who had always been the most independent and outgoing of the girls, the epitome of confidence, was suddenly terrified to spend a night away from home. It was like she was afraid that if she left the house something else would change while she was away.

Meanwhile, five-year-old Tallulah would eat only white food. We tried to steer her toward a better diet by taking away bagels and cream cheese, and she responded by not eating *anything* . . . for days. It was her reaction to things feeling out of control. This was the way a kindergartner was able to find some power, and she was remarkably stubborn. (I finally gave in and let her have the bagels. It may not have been the ideal choice, but I also couldn't let her starve.) I was concerned about her using food as a source of control and where that could lead; I recognized all too well the possibility that this could turn into something bigger. These issues weren't necessarily out of the norm, but if I hadn't been there to address them, they could easily have escalated.

The move to Idaho was best for my girls, but it wasn't easy transitioning to being on my own without the distraction of work. I fought feeling sorry for myself and using the wrong things to push away that feeling. From the beginning, I made a pledge: I would not use alcohol or drugs to get through my divorce, and the same went for food. I remembered what I had put myself through before trying to control *my* body and *my* emotions, and if I gave in to that again, I knew it would destroy me.

Bruce stayed in the guest house in Hailey for a while after we decided to separate. Eventually, he moved into his own house, about ten miles away on the road to Ketchum. When the house and property across the street from us became available, Bruce bought it. We then had a true family compound where the children could easily go back and forth between their parents, and enjoy the luxury of Bruce's heated swimming pool, even in the dead of winter. It was ideal.

It's a funny thing to say, but I'm very proud of our divorce. I think Bruce was fearful at the beginning that I was going to make our split difficult, that I would express my anger or whatever baggage I had from our marriage by obstructing his access to the kids—that I'd turn to all of those ploys divorcing couples use as weapons. But I didn't, and neither did he. I had no desire to replicate the destructive way my parents had used my brother and me as pawns. I'd seen what that could do to people, and I knew from the inside how that felt to be entrapped within as a child.

It wasn't easy at first, but we managed to move the heart of our relationship, the heart of what created our family, into something new that gave the girls a loving, supportive environment with both parents. They were never put in a position of having to choose between us for this holiday or that birthday; we were each able to put our own things aside and share those times with them. I am convinced we would have very different children now if we had handled things more selfishly.

I experienced the most conventional family dynamic I'd ever known in those years. I was the stay-at-home mom whose life revolved entirely around the girls, their schedules, their breaks, their schools, their activities; and Bruce was the one working, the breadwinner. That Bruce was no longer my husband was irrelevant because he was the active father of my children; we felt more connected than we did before the divorce.

Our house in Hailey is a very long ranch, and Rumer's and Scout's rooms were down a long corridor at the other end of the house from the master bedroom. The distance was too scary for them in the dark of night when they were little, so the children slept in the master bedroom for many years. We all piled in together—probably not the best thing for a marriage, but very cozy, and, regardless, that's what we did. After a year or so of continuing that sleeping arrangement when the girls and I were alone in the house, I realized I couldn't even entertain the thought of spending time with someone else unless I could figure out how to get the girls out of my bedroom. It was just too big of a step for Scout and Rumer to go the whole distance to their rooms, and Tallulah only ever slept with me, so I came up with the idea of creating a "sleeping room" near mine: there were three mattresses on the floor and the bedtime essentials—toothbrushes, books, pajamas, music box—and we used the room only at night. For daytime there was the playroom we'd created when we were doing our big renovation. We'd had an intricate birdhouse on a shelf in the living room, and on a whim, I asked one of the carpenters if he could re-create it as a playhouse. The result was an exact replica with a shingled roof, clapboard walls, and Dutch doors. It was enchanting.

There were all sorts of projects to do on the property, which I finally had time for. We had a little playground near the house and as the girls grew, I added more swings and climbing equipment. Their classmates would often come over en masse to play out there. An offshoot of the Big Wood River runs behind the house, and I had stones laid along the shoreline to prevent erosion. When the river was low, the mud was high, and the girls loved to cover themselves with it. When the water was high, the girls swam and tootled around in an inner tube in our backyard pond. Winter comes early in the mountains, and the girls would skate on the river and carve ice caves right off the deck of the house with their friends.

I made good friends of my own in Hailey, who saw me as a neighbor and fellow mom, and nothing more. Scout's dearest friend since she was eighteen months old, Sarah Jane, is the daughter of a hysterically funny, no-nonsense, and totally irreverent woman named Sheri—Sheri-O, we call her—who became (and remains) one of my closest confidants and favorite partners in crime. She is a great golfer, and Bruce used to love spending hours with her on the course. Our girls called themselves Hamster Jane and Skunky LaRue.

Hailey really felt like our home.

MY KIDS GAVE me permission to play. When I wasn't working on the house, I was spending hours putting together American Girl bedroom sets and making forts for stuffed animals. And I had an excuse to shop for toys.

My time to play as a child was very limited, and now I was making up for it with an enthusiasm that verged on obsession. I remember going to the Target in Twin Falls with the girls— Hunter worked some magic so we could stay after hours, and it was amazing being in there on our own; it felt like being at Willy Wonka's Chocolate Factory. Within seconds we had zeroed in on the toy section.

My eyes locked on the Cabbage Patch dolls. I pulled down three supposedly identical variations—to anyone else, they would have all looked like the same doll. But I started scanning back and forth between them, checking which had the sweetest expression, which one had the eyes at the ideal spacing, looking back and forth and back and forth for . . . what?

What was I looking for?

I didn't go to a therapist after Bruce and I split. I bought toys. It was an addiction, but it was also a lifeline: in recent years, as I've cleared out storerooms stuffed with toys and dolls I accumulated during that time, I could feel the pain they held. I realize now that my obsession with collecting kept me from doing something that could have been much worse. At the time, though, I think I would have told you things were good: Bruce and I were getting along. The girls were thriving. I started dating a martial artist I met after he did a demonstration at Scout's eighth birthday party; Oliver gave me the chance to re-discover myself as a woman—not as a wife or mother. For once, I had removed all expectations from a romantic relationship.

Hunter was a constant companion. He was more than an assistant; he was like a member of our family. He had been with me for the most intense period of my career, and for the death of my mother, and now, here he was, walking by my side through the divorce, witnessing my toy-shopping insanity without judgment. Not that he's without a sense of humor: "I'll be nicer if you'll be smarter" is one of my favorite Hunterisms. His sarcastic wit was his funny but loving way of delivering a dose of the truth.

And the truth is what I was after. I think during those years in Idaho, when I stepped away from Hollywood at the peak of my earning power and my success, I was really trying to figure myself out. I had no interest in working. (The only thing I said yes to was a voice-over gig for a Chevy commercial because I was able to do it by driving down the road to a recording studio in Ketchum and then swinging by the girls' school in time for pickup.) I had moments when I thought, *Will I be okay if I never work again? Will this be enough?*

I was searching in all directions for an answer. I read every self-help book I could get my hands on. I met with a Tibetan monk. I worked with a shaman from New Mexico. I had a Cherokee medicine woman come to conduct a ceremony at my house. I went trekking in Bhutan with Oliver. I hosted a weekend workshop exploring the power of intuition and intention with my old friend Laura Day. I was open to finding the truth wherever it might be—and I looked under every spiritual sofa cushion. My quest for insight and meaning *was* my work, at that time.

FOR ALL OF the advantages of living in a small town, it can also be restricting. Rumer, who was finishing elementary school when Bruce and I separated, had a hard time not only with our split-up but with finding a way to fit in socially with her schoolmates. That situation did not improve in middle school; as she was poised to begin high school, she decided she wanted to try something new. In 2002, she started her freshman year at

Interlochen, an arts-focused boarding school in Michigan that's like the Juilliard of high schools. She was the youngest voice major they'd ever accepted.

Around that same time, I got the opportunity to branch out myself. Drew Barrymore called. She was producing a sequel to her movie *Charlie's Angels*, which had been a big hit two years before, starring Cameron Diaz, Drew, and Lucy Liu. She wanted to know if I would consider playing a new character named Madison Lee, a former Angel turned renegade, a good girl gone bad. "The part was written just for you," Drew told me. I liked her a lot—in fact, I liked all the people who were involved with that film. But I was reluctant to leave Hailey and the cocoon I'd created there. Drew didn't give up. "Think about it," she said. "The shooting schedule is only twenty days."

I flew to L.A. to meet with her. "Please trust us," she said to me. "This part is only for you. And it's only for twenty days." For once, there'd be no way for me to start with my usual negative thinking on a film: Drew was begging me to come on board, and my agents were clamoring that this was a great opportunity. It wasn't the project I'd imagined myself stepping back in to do, and I wasn't entirely comfortable with playing a villain. What really pushed me over the edge, though, was how excited my girls were: they'd seen the first *Charlie's Angels*, and the idea of me being in the second had them whipped into a frenzy. We were all ready for some excitement and a change of scene.

CHAPTER 18

I was in New York doing advance press for *Charlie's Angels*, which had been a *completely different experience for me*: really physical, really female, really fun. It was the spring of 2003, and I had just finished shooting the cover of *Vogue* with Mario Testino. My friend Sara Foster called and asked if I wanted to have dinner with a bunch of friends. She mentioned that Ashton Kutcher was going to be there—an actor who'd been on television for a while in *That '70s Show* and whose star was on the rise. He had a surprise hit with a hidden-camera show he'd created himself called *Punk'd*, and he was having a moment—he was in town to host *Saturday Night Live* that weekend.

We all gathered in his hotel room at the start of the evening; he had just finished rehearsal and needed a quick shower. He was prancing around the suite in a towel when I excused myself to call my girls. I was out in the hallway telling them good night when the door opened and Ashton, now fully dressed, leaned out. He looked at me with a serious, almost shy look on his face. "That's the most beautiful thing I've ever heard," he said, then quickly closed the door. In that moment he changed from a cute little player into someone deeply interesting.

That night at dinner, it was like nobody else was there.

He told me about growing up in the cornfields of Iowa. It was clear right away from the way he talked about his goals that he had a serious work ethic, a kind of small-town belief in putting his nose to the grindstone. He was tall and floppy-haired, and, like me, he'd started out his career modeling. But I liked that his handsomeness had something sort of skewed about it: he'd broken his nose a bunch of times, and it gave his face a quirkiness. He was gregarious and warm and animated, and I just felt so much sparkling joy in his company.

When everyone else was ready to go home, we still weren't finished talking. I was staying at my apartment in the San Remo, which I got in the divorce from Bruce. I'd decided to sell it, so there was barely any furniture, just lots of space— three floors!—and stunning views of Central Park. I invited Ashton to come back there with me, and we stayed up the entire night, still talking, telling each other our life stories—and understanding everything the other person was saying. It felt like we were continuing a conversation we'd already been having for years. There was just an ease between us, a deep comfort—and a lot of electricity. It's not every day you meet someone with whom you feel both totally secure and totally stirred up. Eventually, we fell asleep, side by side.

The next day, Ashton had to go to rehearsal for *SNL*, and I had to get back home for a performance Scout was in at school. We continued our conversation digitally: Ashton and I couldn't stop texting. Between every wardrobe change at rehearsal he was texting me, and I couldn't resist replying immediately: it was that level of frenzied attentiveness. We were texting back and forth so much it was like that game where you try to keep a balloon in the air and you don't want to be the one to let it drop.

It was a beautiful clear day, but when I got to the airport that afternoon, it was completely shut down; they said a massive storm—level four—was coming. It was the strangest thing: the sky was sunny, cloudless, and blue, but I literally couldn't leave New York City. It felt like the universe was opening up this window for us, demanding that we spend more time together. Of course I texted Ashton immediately. "You're not going to believe this, but my plane's not taking off. Do you want to hang out?" That night, he texted me between each sketch while they were taking off his wig and stuffing him into the next one, and he came over as soon as he finished the show.

After that, we weren't able to see each other for several weeks. But we were on the phone constantly, totally connected, buzzing with infatuation and excitement. It felt great. When I entered the relationship with Ashton, I had a newfound confidence that my perceptions were clear and strong, and that I *knew* myself—this was the gift from that very centering period in Hailey, away from the action and distraction of L.A. I didn't feel insecure around him. It was the way I'd always wished it could be: love that felt pure and simple and profound. I knew what I wanted more explicitly than I ever had before in my life, and it seemed like maybe life was presenting me with just that: real intimacy. A soul mate.

He was twenty-five. I was forty. But I'm telling you: we couldn't feel it. We were totally in sync, from our very first conversation. Keep in mind, when *I* was twenty-five, I became a mom. I skipped straight from being a young adult into motherhood and marriage. When I met Ashton, it almost felt like a do-over, like I could just go back in time and experience what it was like to be young, with him—much more so than I'd ever been able to experience it when I was actually in my twenties.

And it's not like he was some flaky kid. He had a very mature approach to life. He had a bigger picture in his mind: at twenty-five, he was already extremely focused on his future. He was—and still is—the hardest worker I've ever met. That was uplifting and dynamic to be around.

A few weeks after that first meeting, Ashton and I finally had a chance to see each other again in Los Angeles. We had spent so much time on the phone talking by then, it was almost overwhelming to see him in person. Just the touch of his hand was electric, because there was already so much emotion behind it. We went to In-N-Out Burger, trying to avoid paparazzi and keep things low key. I knew, from day one, that if Ashton and I got together, it would be a feeding frenzy. It was just too juicy with our age difference, with me having been out of the public eye and Ashton being very much in it at that moment because *Punk'd* was such a thing. I tried to warn him about what was coming if we became a couple. I told him, "You will be followed. They will be *everywhere*. That ease of movement you're used to? It will be a thing of the past." But he didn't really take it in. How could he? He later confessed that if he'd fully grasped what it would be like, he might never have gotten involved with me.

After dinner that night, he took me to see a piece of land he'd bought just below Mulholland Drive in the mountains above Beverly Hills, where he wanted to build his dream house some-day. I loved that he was such an expansive thinker who seemed to look at life in its entirety, who wasn't just reacting to whatever came his way. It was another perfect night, one that I'll never forget. Maybe because I was older and more self-assured than I'd been in previous relationships, or maybe because I'd finally made peace with my body, or maybe just because of the inherent nature of our dynamic, but for whatever reason, I felt completely safe with Ashton, which made it possible to connect sexually in a way I'd never experienced before.

That sense of security also enabled me to be emotionally vulnerable and open in a new way. I had completely shut out the memory of that awful experience with Val when I was fifteen; I didn't even know to file it under "rape" in my own mind. I just knew it haunted me. That whenever I was in a situation where I felt vulnerable, the fifteen-year-old me was who showed up. Ashton was the first person I really talked to about that, and it allowed me to start dealing with that trauma, that shame, and to start healing.

He had a night off, and he decided to fly back to Idaho with me, to see my life there. Hunter and Sheri-O, who happened to be in L.A., were flying out to Hailey with me, and as we were driving to the airport, I told Sheri, "I have a secret: I'm kind of going out with Ashton Kutcher." Sheri said, "I have absolutely no idea who that is." We pulled over to a newsstand and Hunter jumped out and bought a *Rolling Stone*, which had Ashton on the cover. When Sheri looked at it, she said, "Well, he's certainly hot enough!" And I certainly agreed.

Ashton was very shy when we all met up at the airport and got on the jet that Bruce and I still shared. In fact, he was so nervous he barely spoke a word during the entire flight. I was reminded of the first time I went on a private plane with Bruce early in our relationship, and how thrilling and strange that had been. When we landed in Hailey, we went to go pick up our girls: Scout and Sheri's daughter Sarah Jane were just getting back from a school trip to a wilderness survival course. Ashton turned to me in the car and said, "I want you to know, I don't take coming into a kid's life lightly. I know it's not something you can just come in and out of."

When the girls got off the bus and saw us, they all started whispering, "Is that ASHTON KUTCHER?!?"

He clicked with Scout and Tallulah right away. Ashton had a wonderful stepfather who meant a lot to him, so I think he innately understood the impact that men could have on the lives of children who weren't biologically theirs. And he *liked* that I was a mom: I think the possibility of being someone important to my kids was a part of the relationship that appealed to him. That might sound like an odd thing for a twenty-five-year-old, but again, he wasn't your average young guy. On the one hand, he was naughty and scampish, but on the other, there was a responsible, sincere, and centered quality to him. He had a very strong sense of the role that a good man should play in the life of a family. And he wanted to be part of our gang.

The next day, our plane had to return to L.A. to get Bruce, and Ashton went with it to get back to his job. I wanted Bruce to know in case they crossed paths—I told him, "I have a friend who'll be getting off the plane, Ashton Kutcher." Bruce's reaction was: "You are *such* a good mom." He assumed I'd brought Ashton as a special treat for the girls, the way we'd once arranged for Aaron Carter to come to Disney World for Scout's birthday.

AS IT TURNED out, Ashton and Bruce got along really well. We hung out regularly, playing cards, having dinner, just chilling out. It was lovely. (A funny aside: Ashton first moved to L.A. with January Jones, the actress who played Betty Draper on *Mad Men*. They were engaged, and they were both just starting out at the time—modeling, taking small parts. As a twenty-three-year-old, January had a tiny role in the movie *Bandits*, which Bruce starred in when he was forty-six. Ashton was convinced they'd had a fling on set. Years later, I happened to sit next to January at an event, and I mentioned this. "Are you *serious*?" she said, laughing. "I told him a hundred times, I didn't want to fuck that old man!")

Ashton and I kept our relationship quiet for a little while, but then it just got silly: we were in love, and we wanted to be in each other's lives for everything, big and small. In June 2003, we made our first public appearance together, at the premiere of *Charlie's Angels: Full Throttle*. In a fantastic Missoni mini-dress, I took on the red carpet, with Ashton on one arm and Bruce on the other, and all three kids front and center. I was saying, *You can be a family after divorce, just in a new form.* And I was preemptively neutralizing any narrative of conflict between Bruce and Ashton the press might try to drum up. It worked. It was a damn good night.

But the response to our relationship was every bit as frenzied as I'd anticipated, maybe even more so. We were in the tabloids constantly; we couldn't leave the house without being photographed. My agents said that my relationship was hurting me: all the focus on me being with a younger man meant that people weren't taking me seriously. I didn't care. I'd never been so happy in my life.

I bought a beautiful house, not far from that piece of land where he wanted to build his dream house, up in the mountains above Beverly Hills. It was like a peaceful Zen tree house, high above the noise and traffic of the city. You could watch the sun set pink over the mountains when you sat out back by the pool, and you could see the trees everywhere you looked through the glass walls. It was going to be our oasis.

Ashton and I didn't want to be apart for a minute. When my house was being renovated, he invited my girls and me to stay with him. It just seemed foolish to go rent something separate when we wanted to be together all the time, and the girls loved Ashton. Rumer wanted to come back to L.A.: she missed her family, and boarding school hadn't been all it was cracked up to be.

Ashton's house was one of his first big purchases, high above Beverly Hills, complete with tennis courts and a pool—it was a pretty remarkable place for a twenty-five-year-old to have earned. Ashton had a very different relationship with success than Bruce had. He didn't spend wildly. He was careful and methodical, and his investments always reflected that, including his first home. Though prior to our arrival, it had been a straight-up L.A. party house—you can read about it in *Rolling Stone*. (George Bush was president at the time, and somehow his twin daughters ended up doing bong hits at that house at one of Ashton's parties. He was sure the Secret Service was listening in on his calls from then on.) There were definitely some late-night doorbell rings before word got out about Ashton's new roommates.

About a year and a half into our relationship, Ashton hosted *SNL* for a second time, and we decided to address all the chatter about our age difference head-on, and in the funniest way possible. Unlike the time I'd hosted alone, this time I enjoyed every minute. During his opening monologue, Ashton said, "Magazines focus on our age difference, and all that I focus on is she is the best thing that has ever happened to me, and she's here tonight. Demi, I love you, baby." The camera panned to me in the audience—in makeup that made me look about ninety, with a white wig and eyebrows, wearing a frowsy purple dress and holding a pocketbook in my lap like the Queen of England. "You're doin' great, baby," I croaked in my best old-lady voice. "You're lookin' hot!"

Then Ashton called me up to the stage "so we can just enjoy this moment together," and I shuffled out of my seat and leaned over onto the walker that was waiting for me in the aisle. "She is still the hottest woman in Hollywood," he announced once I was up onstage, which got a huge laugh because I looked like I had just hobbled out of a nursing home, and I had these massive, hanging boobs the *SNL* people had made for me. "I wear this medallion as a symbol of our love," Ashton said, gesturing to his necklace. I followed that up with, "And I've got this identification bracelet; it lets the medical technicians know I've got the di- abetes!" Ashton nodded and said, "She's got 'em bad." Then we made out a little and my false teeth came out in his mouth.

The whole thing was hilarious. I loved that I was at a point in my life where I didn't care what the tabloids said; I didn't care what people thought of my choices. I was living the way *I* wanted to live. And there was no reason to be sensitive about my age: I had just turned forty-two. And I was pregnant.

CHAPTER 19

Ashton and I knew right away that we wanted to have a baby together, it was always just a question of when. I had leapt into having a family with Bruce, and this time, I wanted to build a foundation in the relationship first. I wanted time for us to enjoy each other. But I was also in my forties. To remove the time pressure, less than a year into our relationship, we decided to freeze embryos.

I was offered a movie called *Half Light*, which was supposed to be the big follow-up my team had gotten for me on the heels of *Charlie's Angels*. I'm sure most of you have never even heard of it, which tells you something. It was an interesting script—a thriller/ghost story about a bestselling crime novelist who is haunted by guilt over the accidental death of her son—but there were issues with money, the director was unknown, and shooting it would mean being away from my girls for a month before they could come see me—longer than we'd ever been apart.

Ashton told me to do it. "The girls will stay here, and I'll come home for dinner every night," he said. "I will hold down family life, as if you'd never left."

We filmed in Wales and Cornwall. Before I left L.A., I had given in and bought all three girls devices, so they could reach me anytime they wanted. Technology had just gotten to the point where everyone was texting photos back and forth, and I missed my girls and Ashton terribly, though they seemed happy in the flow of pictures we exchanged. I was elated when he brought them to see me. We stayed in an amazing house in London, near Mayfair, that had once been a nunnery. There was a pool in the basement—it was like going swimming in an underground cave. It was such an adventure exploring all the back staircases with the girls and figuring out what went where in that crazy house.

One night, after they'd gone to bed, Ashton and I sat in the great room, cross-legged on the floor in front of the fireplace, and had our first conversation about getting married. We were so comfortable, sitting in that gorgeous firelight, and it was a really mellow, easy conversation about whether we ought to consider it for my girls. Was it something that might be helpful for them, we wondered, as they tried to make sense of this new family, our new household? There was so much press about our relationship not being serious, when, in fact, he had just come from holding down the fort for a month; the girls had started calling him MOD, short for "my other dad."

Ashton and I went to a Shabbat service at the Kabbalah Centre in Marylebone. I had begun studying Kabbalah soon after I moved back from Idaho. When I'd first arrived back in L.A., I felt like I didn't know anyone anymore. But my friend Guy Oseary, who I've been close with since the nineties, was there, and he got me back into the social swing of things: he took me to dinner parties; took me to clubs (I didn't drink, but I loved to dance); reconnected me to Madonna—her husband at the time, Guy Ritchie, gave me a copy of *The Power of Kabbalah*. Guy Oseary then invited me to come and meet their teacher, Eitan, at the Beverly Hills offices of Maverick, the record label he'd started with Madonna, and it was a deeply calm and insightful hour, hearing Eitan speak about the tenets of Kabbalah and the spiritual side of Judaism. I was curious to know more, so I went home and jumped into reading the book. Madonna was doing a weekly class at her house, and I started to go regularly.

When Ashton and I got together, he became interested in Kabbalah, too. We shared a yearning for a spiritual life. He was raised Catholic; I was baptized Catholic but raised not much of anything. But we were both really questioning what we were meant to be and do, how we fit into the grand plan. We were convinced that, however that was, our union was a step on the right path.

The girls were seventeen, fourteen, and eleven at the time, and, as I've said, he really wanted to be the world's greatest stepdad. He was also a vibrant guy in his twenties who wanted to go out and have fun, and we did a lot of that, too. We went to Lakers games; we hung out with his friends from *That '70s Show*; I introduced him to everyone I knew in L.A., which by then was a pretty wide swath of the entertainment industry.

Ashton was very good at connecting with people—networking, to use an old-fashioned word for it. He was good at it in person, and he was good at it online. He was one of the first people to have more than a million Twitter followers; he understood the power of social media way before most people, and he got me into it for a while, too. Originally, Ashton and I were just playing, seeing what it did and what it meant. But then I realized that Twitter was a way for me to interact directly with people without the media middlemen. I think people had seen a disproportionate number of pictures of me in the tabloids frowning or looking angry as I tried to ward off the omnipresent circling photographers; I saw Twitter as an opportunity to show people a side of myself that is much lighter and warmer. And all of a sudden people were getting to know *me*, not a tabloid image of "Gimme Moore" or whoever the press had decided I was that week. I was connecting with them, sharing something real. And it was a two-way street. Once, when Ashton was out of the country, and he knew I was asleep, he sent out a message to all his followers to start a "love tsunami" by flooding my Twitter feed with messages of love all at the same time. I was still in my pajamas when I noticed my Sidekick—the device of the moment—was blowing up with thousands of love tweets.

Ashton was great about stuff like that. He left Post-it Notes around the house with messages like "Remember you are magical" or just plain old "I love you," and they meant so much to me that some of them stayed up for five or six years. It was such a gift to live with someone who so clearly wanted me to feel good, to have fun, to experience pleasure.

He took me to Mexico for a romantic Valentine's Day trip, complete with a rose petal path leading through the master suite to a candlelit tub. This was our first solo vacation together, and we really went for it. We had couples' massages, and read together under a canopy on the beach. But most of the time we just lounged naked in bed.

One night, we put some clothes on and went out to dinner. Ashton was enjoying a glass of good red wine when he said, "I don't know if alcoholism is a real thing—I think it's all about moderation."

I wanted to be that girl. The girl who could have a glass of wine at dinner, or do a tequila shot at a party. In my mind, Ashton wanted that, too. So I tried to become that: a fun, normal girl. I didn't think, *This is a kid in his twenties who has no idea what he's talking about.* I didn't think, *I have nearly two decades of sobriety under my belt, and that's a huge accomplishment.* Instead, I cast about for justifications for his argument. *Plenty of people party too much in their youth and then develop a perfectly healthy relationship with alcohol,* I told myself. I used food as a way to torture myself at one point, and since then I had changed my relationship with eating—but obviously without giving it up altogether. Could I do that with alcohol, too? Back in our room, I took a beer from the minibar.

That first weekend when I opened the door to alcohol again, it was such a novelty to have a buzz. And that's all it was—I had this under control, I told myself. We left Mexico and flew to Chicago, where Ashton was taping *Oprah*. I was watching from the greenroom as he gushed about me during the taping—I could see the women in the audience swooning.

We went to Florida next, for a big NASCAR race in Daytona, where Ashton was the honorary starter. There was a hotel room set up for us to use during the race. I slipped back into the room by myself and dipped into the minibar for a beer. No one was monitoring me, of course, but I couldn't shake the feeling that I was doing something wrong—you can't be sober for twenty years and not feel like you're going to get in trouble if you have a drink. The words AA uses to describe alcoholism are *cunning, baffling,* and *powerful. Can I really get away with this?* I thought. *If I just drink beer?* I drank it all weekend in furtive, deliberate sips.

Our final stop was Miami, where Sean Combs had offered us his house on the Intracoastal Waterway—it was incredibly beautiful, and it was just the two of us. It was there that I noticed my period was late, and I mentioned it to Ashton. "Although we've been traveling and sometimes that throws things off . . ." I hedged. There was nobody we could send to the drugstore to get a test, and no way either of us could risk buying one ourselves. But I already knew in my gut. It was a long and exciting twenty-four hours.

I sent Hunter a message, and he had a test waiting for me at the house when we got back to L.A. the next day. When I saw the plus sign come up, I was in shock, then excited, then worried, and then I worked through the whole cycle of emotions all over again. But when I told Ashton, his reaction overrode my mixed emotions: he was thrilled.

Six weeks later, in Parrot Cay, he proposed. He asked me to go down to the beach to watch the sunset, and then he got down on one knee and presented me with a beautiful vintage Cartier ring. I was overwhelmed. I told him I needed to think about it. I didn't want him to feel he had to marry me just because I was pregnant. But I loved him. And I knew he loved me. And I knew this baby would cement our family, bond us all on the deepest level.

By the end of the night, I'd said yes.

Recently, I happened to see an old clip of myself on an episode of *Late Show with David Letterman*. It was from 1994, and I was there to promote the movie *Disclosure*. Letterman said, "You just got a great life! You have a storybook life." It was soon after Tallulah had been born, and he talked about my beautiful daughters. "And you're a beautiful woman," he continued. "You couldn't be more successful, you've got a husband who's doing okay," he joked, "and every movie that you're in turns out to be not only a good movie but very, very successful." Some of that was, of course, hyperbole—a host flattering his guest to make her feel comfortable and to draw her out for the cameras. But some of it was simply the truth. I *did* have three great kids. I had a handsome, famous husband who was, indeed, doing okay. Many of my own films had done well at the box office. I was, without question, fortunate beyond measure. But I was still wracked with self-doubt and insecurity. The life around me was remarkable; the messages in my head were still pretty dark. A decade later, when I found myself engaged to my soul mate and expecting his child at forty-two, I felt, for the first time, like the luckiest girl in the world. I was finally at a point where I could take in all this abundance, truly appreciate it, and truly enjoy it.

We started shopping for the nursery. My friend Soleil Moon Frye—whose husband was Ashton's producing partner at the time—was pregnant, too, and we were excited to be in this together; to have a ready-made circle of new-parent friends.

It was a girl. We named her Chaplin Ray, after a woman I met in Spain, who was my interpreter when I was doing press for *G.I. Jane*. I loved the name and I loved my newest baby girl.

WITH EACH PREGNANCY, a woman tends to look bigger faster, and when I was pregnant with Chaplin I became colossal. We kept it totally hidden; only Bruce and the girls and our closest inner circle knew that I was pregnant. I didn't want my youngest daughter to come into the world as tabloid fodder.

And thank God.

Almost six months into my pregnancy, right at the moment when we were going to start telling everyone, we went to the doctor's office. He did his usual ultrasound, but this time, there was no heartbeat. I registered that deadly silence—instead of the now-familiar thump*thump!* thump*thump!* of Chaplin's little heart—and saw the look on my doctor's face.

If you have never lost a baby, you may think of a miscarriage as not that big a deal. It's hard to remember, but I'm sure I used to feel that way, too: like it was a bit of medical misfortune, a disappointing but not devastating setback. But when it is *your* baby, who you already love and think of as a member of your immediate family, it doesn't feel like a minor defeat. It feels like your child has died.

I was decimated. I shifted into survival mode. I tried to allow myself to mourn, but it was so confusing. How could I grieve a person who'd never been in the world? I didn't even know who she was. I just knew that I wanted her back with every molecule of my being.

Ashton did his best to connect with me in my grief. He tried to be there for me during the miscarriage, but he couldn't really understand what I was feeling. First of all, he hadn't carried this baby. And second, he was in his *twenties* at the time: he wasn't remotely late to the game of fatherhood. His possibilities were not running out, far from it. I was suddenly acutely aware that mine were. I had been very lucky to get pregnant naturally in my forties. I was terrified that I wouldn't be able to do it again. I had literally failed to deliver, and my grief felt bottomless. I went through the motions of life, but I don't know that I was fully in it.

I recently came across a note that Tallulah wrote me at the time. It said, "I'm really sorry you lost the baby. But I'm still here. And I love you."

IT WAS MY fault, I felt sure: if only I hadn't opened the door to drinking, I never would have lost the baby. Even worse, I was still smoking when I found out I was pregnant, and it took me a few weeks to quit completely. I was wracked with guilt and convinced what had happened was my doing.

Drinking became interwoven in my pain. *I've had a devastating experience, I'm drinking, that's okay.* That's what I told myself. But somewhere inside of me, I knew that there was nothing okay about the way I related to alcohol.

Ashton, meanwhile, was back in his empire-building mode. I was just with myself—not working, replaying over and over again what I did and what I missed during my pregnancy that could have made this happen.

But I still had a glimmer of hope. I could try again. *Now we know we want this, it's really clear, let's get on with it!*

We decided to get married. Our Kabbalah teacher suggested it would be healing—that it would deepen our connection, uniting two souls as one. I threw myself into planning the wedding.

THERE WAS CHATTER early on that our relationship was just an elaborate publicity stunt. It was ridiculously difficult for people to believe an older woman and a younger man could actually be happily in love—though nobody blinks an eye when the situation is reversed. (Bruce and his wife, for example, have a twenty-three-year age difference, and nobody's ever made a peep.) But by the time Ashton and I got married on September 24, 2005, we'd already been through a lot of real challenges as a couple in the two years we had been together. It didn't feel like we were rushing into anything, quite the contrary. We were celebrating a love that had already survived trial by fire.

I went through herculean efforts to keep our wedding private, with the help of Hunter and Ashton's dad, Larry. The guest list was small, just our closest friends and family, and most of them thought they were coming over for a housewarming party. The renovations on our Zen tree house had just been completed, and we had the ceremony there, in our living room. It was as intimate and low key as my wedding to Bruce had been big and over the top. Ashton's father and his mom and stepdad came, along with his twin brother, Michael; his big sister, Tausha; and his niece, Dakota. Bruce was there, with the girls, of course, and, representing my family, George and DeAnna, and Morgan. Lucy Liu arrived after the ceremony was already under way and snuck to her seat with an expression of shock and delight on her face, housewarming gift under one arm.

I wore a beautiful, simple ivory Lanvin gown my friend Alber Elbaz had magically made for me in just a few weeks' time. Ashton wore white too, for our traditional Kabbalistic ceremony under a chuppah. I walked around Ashton seven times to symbolize the circle of love, and he smashed a glass with his foot—a reminder of the fragility of relationships. Of how easy it can be to break them to pieces.

CHAPTER 20

We did everything together. We loved playing games, and one of our favorites was Mexican train dominoes—we started doing that two or three nights a week, and we played by the Salma Hayek rules: everyone's train comes from the same central line of dominoes, and you're in a cutthroat struggle to block your opponents. Penelope Cruz and her roommate, Daya, introduced us to the game; Heather, Guy, and sometimes Bruce would come, and our friend Eric Buterbaugh, who did the flowers for our wedding. We had a weekly Kabbalah class at our house on Wednesdays; TJ, Ashton's old roommate, and the rest of their fantasy football league came on Sundays. We had family dinners together every night—Ashton organized his schedule around them. All of the friends coming and going felt like part of our extended family.

Every year, we all went to Parrot Cay the day after Christmas.

It was a ritual I started with Bruce: we'd get up and ski in the mountains in Idaho in the morning, and then get on a plane and be swimming in the ocean by nightfall. It was there that I drank in front of the girls for the first time, at the bar by the swimming pool. I ordered a beer. Ashton ordered a cocktail. I was mindful of how much I was having at first, vigilant about how I was feeling. And then our new friend at the bar—Fratboy Phil, we were calling him—said: "Have you ever chugged a beer through a straw?" We had a competition to see who could do it fastest, and I won. We repeated this process three times. It didn't occur to me that Phil was six feet four inches and probably three times my weight. I was hammered. In the golf cart on the way back to our room, I was slumped in the front seat and Rumer was laughing about how silly I was being. "Oh Mom, I love you," she said, to which I drunkenly replied, "I feel the same."

It was funny to them when I drank that time. But it didn't stay funny. I had always been so careful with my kids to be stable, even-keeled, gentle, even in the way I casually addressed them. When you drink you become more direct and uninhibited— or at least I do—and to them, compared to the way I'd been throughout their childhood, I sounded harsher. And it was just new, different: they'd never seen me, or adults generally, partying. I remember at Rumer's sixteenth birthday party, Tallulah was terrified because some of the people were drunk, and it was so unfamiliar to her she didn't know what to make of it. But I was able to reassure and comfort her: I was still her same old mom, and she would always be safe with me.

ASHTON AND I still wanted to have a baby, and we thoroughly enjoyed trying the old-fashioned way. But after a few months, we threw in a little intrauterine insemination, just to be safe. When that hadn't worked after a year, we moved on to IVF.

The daily shots and constant trips to the doctor's office that in vitro fertilization requires can make even a young woman feel desperate and out of control. I didn't care for our first doctor, who kept emphasizing my age. We found another fertility specialist I liked a lot, and I did fairly well with the hormones.

But every time I got my period, proof that another cycle had failed, I felt myself reliving Chaplin's death, and I went into a terribly dark place.

I kept that completely secret. I soldiered on. From the outside, I looked like my usual optimistic, practical self. Inside, I was dying.

On paper there was no reason why I shouldn't have been getting pregnant. I was making plenty of eggs. They were fertilizing. But it just wasn't happening. I must have gone through four or five cycles, all of which ended in heartbreak. Every time, you get your hopes up. You're getting shots in your stomach and your butt every morning and every night. You're constantly getting ultrasounds and having your blood drawn to find out when you're ovulating, when your uterine lining is just right, and so on. You're organizing your whole life around getting pregnant, and when you find out that—yet again—you're not, it's crushing. It takes a toll on a woman when you spend years of your life in that state.

To his credit, Ashton was fine with having a baby however: we could use a surrogate, or we could use a donor egg. But my ego was attached to having a biological child I carried. That's what I'd always done before. Intellectually, I knew that one can connect with a baby on the deepest level without carrying her. But emotionally, I wanted to have that experience with Ashton. Just as I wanted to be the carefree girl who could have a casual drink, I wanted to be the fertile woman who could have his baby. I was starting to worry that maybe I *was*, as the tabloids so kindly reminded the world at every chance, past my sell-by date.

Throughout the course of this awful period, I think I began to take my relationships with my daughters for granted. Obviously, I wasn't going to bother them with the details of my IVF; it wouldn't have been appropriate. But to them, I had become secretive. In Idaho, they'd felt like we were all in it together, but now it seemed like Ashton and I were shutting them out. To make things even more complicated, they were at the age when kids naturally start to separate from their parents. And as teenagers, Rumer and Scout were racing with hormones, while I was pumped full of them from my IVF.

Ultimately, I assumed that our bond was safe no matter what. When your kids stop looking like kids—they look big and they act big—it can be easy to lose sight of the fact that they will forever see you through the eyes of a child. I think that in my pain, I may have lost sight of how much mothering they still needed.

ASHTON WAS GETTING ready to do a movie called *Spread*. It was clear from the script it would be *very* sexual—even graphic. Jennifer Jason Leigh was slated to play the female lead, and one day Ashton came home from the office and told me, "Jennifer is concerned about you being on set." He seemed really uneasy and told me how much it could hurt his career if she was displeased: she was married at the time to the director Noah Baumbach, who had a big movie just out. "I might want to work with him someday," Ashton said. "He might not ever cast me because of this." I was mortified. Jennifer and I had the same manager, and I called him, frantic, and said, "*Please* let her know I'd never do anything to compromise the film, and I'd never want to make another actor uncomfortable while she's working!"

My manager called her, then called me back. "Jennifer has absolutely no problem with any of this—she has no issue, and she had no idea what I was talking about."

I was baffled. And talking to Ashton didn't exactly clear

things up. He chalked it up to miscommunication, but something didn't feel right. The bottom line was that *she* wasn't worried about me being on set, *he* was.

I was devastated. Bruce always felt that he wasn't needed, that I gave him *too much* space. I'd been trying not to repeat that mistake. I thought I was being supportive, there for Ashton in whatever he needed—I had gone to stay with him on location in Louisiana while he was shooting *The Guardian* a few months earlier, just to be there for him—but, in fact, what he'd needed was space. And he hadn't told me. He'd only been able to communicate what he wanted by dissembling.

He wasn't honest. That's on him. But I had made him the focus of all my attention and was putting too much pressure on him. I was losing myself. And that's on me.

UNLIKE WHAT PEOPLE imagine about addicts—that you have one drink and everything comes crashing down—in my case it was a gradual downward spiral. The decline in my sense of confidence mirrored my substance abuse.

My agent had recommended renting Joe Francis's house in Puerto Vallarta for my forty-fifth birthday. It's an unbelievable place, run like a six-star hotel. (There's an "anything" button on the phone.) Ashton and I chartered a plane and flew a dozen friends down for the weekend.

Everyone was having a great time and really cutting loose.

We had a huge dinner at the long banquet table; waiters were coming around with trays of tequila shots, and people were getting up on the table and strutting down the middle—our friend Eric did it in nothing but underpants and a pair of pointy-toed boots.

But when you don't have an off switch, you go until you can't go anymore. Late that night, we all ended up in the hot tub, and I started passing out and slipping under the water. If other people hadn't been there, I would have drowned.

Ashton carried me back to our bed, and he was furious. To some extent, I understand his reaction. If this had been the first time something like this had happened, that would have been one thing, but it wasn't.

But it was also confusing: Ashton had encouraged me to go in this direction. When I went too far, though, he let me know how he felt by showing a picture he'd taken of me resting my head on the toilet the night before. It seemed like a good-natured joke at the time. But it was really just shaming.

I WENT IN for dental surgery. I left with a prescription for Vicodin. I took it as I needed it, when I was in bad pain. At first. Then, sometimes, when I wasn't really in pain, I'd think, *Hmm, maybe I'll just take half a pill.* I had back pain at the time, too, and I managed to get another prescription to deal with that. Initially, the pills took the edge off, made life feel just a little bit easier. Whereas alcohol felt risky—I never knew how much was too much—with pills I was in control. They gave me energy to jump in and get things done. Over time, though, they stopped having the same effect, and I needed more and more of them to feel the way I wanted. I got to the point where I was taking twelve a day.

I stopped after I scared myself one weekend when the whole family was together and I lost track of how many pills I'd taken. All of a sudden, I felt like I couldn't breathe.

I told no one. But the next day I had a conversation with Ashton about it, and he asked me if I needed help. I told him I would take care of it myself—and I did.

He was in Europe the following week, and the girls were with their dad. I used that time to detox. It was one of the hardest things I've ever had to do in my entire life. Going off of opiates is agony—it's unimaginably excruciating. You can't sleep because your body hurts too much. It's an effort just to get to the toilet. Your whole body is screaming, "I'm dying: if you just took a *little*, all this pain would go away!" It is like the worst flu you've ever had times a hundred. I gutted through that week.

When Ashton returned home, I felt like I'd lived through a war. He did not offer me any reinforcement or compassion. I felt like he was angry with me for having this problem in the first place: you made your bed; now you have to lie in it.

CHAPTER 21

Ashton was less and less present. He was focused on other things: his work; his growing involvement in the tech world; his fantasy football league. He couldn't have been clearer that whatever he was doing was really important—and I don't fault him for that. But I do wish I'd been able to value myself in the same way.

Instead, I went into contortions to try to fit the mold of the woman he wanted his wife to be. I put him first. He didn't ask me to do that. It's just what I did—what I'd learned to do from my mother, and her mother before her. I wanted this marriage to work, and I was willing to do whatever it took, to jump through any hoop. So when he expressed his fantasy of bringing a third person into our bed, I didn't say no. I wanted to show him how great and fun I could be.

Having other people in our marriage presented a totally

false sense of power, and an absolutely temporary sense of excitement. There were two different people we opened our relationship to, and they didn't have bad intentions; they held it in the right space. To this day, I know I could reach out to either of them at any time for friendship; one is now married and has a kid. They were good people, but it was still a mistake. Part of the point of monogamy is the energy of somebody making the sacrifice or the choice for *you*, and that you thereby hold this special place that no one else can have. As soon as another person is brought in you are no longer being held in that sacred spot.

I WAS WORKING in New York on a film with Ellen Barkin called *Another Happy Day* when the story broke. Ashton had slept with a twenty-one-year-old, in our home, while I was out of town.

I remember the night they met. We were at a bowling alley with Rumer, and when he went to switch out our shoes, she gave him her number on a napkin. Or that's what he told me at the time. When we got home that night and he showed it to me, I said, "That is just *gross*. We were there with our kid, and she was there with her mother and her sister!" I had a visceral response—it was revulsion. So the fact that he then pursued her felt like a real "fuck you."

Suddenly, his infidelity was all over the celebrity gossip

circuit—the young woman even tried to sell a sweater of his on eBay for five hundred dollars.

When the news came out in the press, we were already scheduled to do an event at the Clinton Global Initiative, launching our foundation to fight human trafficking. We had put in over a year researching the issue and setting up the infrastructure. Ashton is a really gifted big-picture thinker; to me, of course, the issue was personal. There was no question of postponing this event.

I went into lockdown mode. I knew how I reacted would be the benchmark for how the tabloid stories would be received. If we had a united front, maybe they would dismiss the whole incident as a shakedown. Maybe the best call was simply to absorb what had happened and ignore it.

So he came to New York and I put on a brave face and we gave our presentation on September 23, 2010—the day before our anniversary. Ashton spoke about how there are more slaves on earth now than in any other time in human history, and detailed our efforts to get Twitter and other Internet platforms to avoid being used as marketplaces for the selling of human beings. I talked about the "Real Men Don't Buy Girls" campaign we were launching, to try to alter the culture that enables men to feel okay about paying for sex with underage girls. "One in five men have engaged in the commercial sex trade," I announced to that room full of important people, standing next to my husband of five years who'd just cheated on me with a girl about the age of my oldest daughter. "Real men protect, respect, love, and care for girls." But I did not feel protected, respected, loved, or cared for myself.

Rumer, who'd moved out on her own by this point and was working as an actor, came with Ashton, which we'd planned long before any of this happened, and then the three of us went to Providence, Rhode Island, to visit Scout, who had recently started at Brown University. I felt strongly that we shouldn't lie to them—and, technically, I didn't—but I allowed them to assume that all the chatter in the tabloids was baseless. My intention was to protect them, but now I see that was a mistake. I cheated *them* out of the opportunity to process this upset with me, as a family. They deserved to know the truth.

Ashton and I decided to drive back to L.A. so we could have the time together, alone. I was strangely flooded with shame; I couldn't shake the feeling that this whole thing was somehow my fault. Because we had brought a third party into our relationship, Ashton said, that blurred the lines and, to some extent, justified what he'd done. I think he felt remorse, but he was also looking for a way to deflect blame, to maintain his own perception of himself as a decent family guy.

Ashton did not compensate for his behavior by being extra solicitous and kind. In retrospect, I think all of this was his way of trying to get out of our marriage. He didn't know how to do that in a loving way, or maybe he was too conflicted. I think part of him cherished what we had; part of him couldn't wait to move on. You can't blame someone for not having the skills or the level of awareness it takes to behave compassionately.

That was the best that he could do. Every one of his actions was saying, *Please don't love me.* But, unfortunately for both of us, I did.

TALLULAH, MY ONLY kid still at home with us, had just turned seventeen and was going through an age-appropriate rebellious phase. One evening in the spring of 2011, she told me she was going to spend the evening with some friends studying for a practice SAT, and I went out to a movie. My phone started ringing in the middle of it: it was another parent I knew. Tallulah and some of her friends had been busted for underage drinking. They were walking into a friend's house carrying a water bottle full of vodka, and it was past curfew in that area, and they'd drawn the attention of the police. I needed to go and pick her up from the station in Hollywood.

When I got there, I made a beeline to the officer in charge and said, "Look: this is obviously not okay, but it's a first of-fense. Can they get off with just a warning here, and we will make sure this never happens again?" His response was: "It'll be off her record when she turns eighteen." But it would never come off of *her* "record" in the public eye in the same way it would for her friends: she would be forever associated with this incident; potential employers would see it the first time they googled her. I've said to my kids for years: it doesn't matter who you're with or what the circumstances are. It will always come out in the press as "Tallulah Willis, busted." Because of who your parents are, you will be subjected to a different kind of scrutiny than your peers; any mistake you make will become news. And that's exactly what happened with the drinking incident. It was all over *TMZ* the next day—just as I feared it would be.

I didn't hug Tallulah when I first saw her at the station, and maybe I should have. I was upset that she had lied to me about where she was going to be that night, and I was focused on trying to convince the cops to keep this quiet. I was trying to protect her. She interpreted that as me caring only about how the whole thing looked.

Teenagers do stupid stuff. But what I saw was that how we handled the incident was going to affect her use of drugs and alcohol going forward. I was a bit tough on her. Bruce wasn't around that weekend; Ashton was away, too. I was the only one there, and I had to leave for a charity event in New York two days later.

In retrospect, I shouldn't have gone. I should have stayed and worked through what had happened with Tallulah. But I went, and she stayed with Emma, who had married Bruce a couple of years earlier. When I returned, I came home to a note that Tallulah didn't want to come back *ever* and would not talk to me.

She was a teenager, pushing boundaries, seeing what she could get away with. That's normal. What wasn't normal at all was that from that point on, it was like everyone in the family was siding with her. Suddenly, Scout didn't want to talk to me, either. Mysteriously, she too "needed space." Bruce refused to discuss the situation with me or to negotiate an appropriate way of addressing what had happened with Tallulah. *I* was being treated like the one who'd had to be picked up in Hollywood from the police! It was baffling.

Of course, everyone had their own reason. Scout was trying to separate, grow up, start a new life at college, and I guess this felt like an opportunity to assert her independence. Bruce was starting a new life with Emma and was not in the mood to deal with his old one. Tallulah was angry about being told what to do. She was just being a kid, but her opinion became everyone's opinion: that I was to blame for a rapidly widening rift.

I think the part that was real was that the girls were angry I'd become so dependent on Ashton—I was addicted to him, is the best way I can put it. And I did all the things that addicts do. I prioritized my addiction over my needs and the needs of my family. I made strange, unconvincing justifications for my behavior—and his. I had held the family together as a pillar, and the pillar was crumbling.

Having two of my daughters not speaking to me was new and unprecedented and awful. It threatened the thing I was proudest of, my role as a mom. And I just plain missed my kids. Ashton was angry; he felt that I had hurt his relationship with the girls. But he still seemed to be trying really hard to be supportive. He sent me a beautiful, reassuring email that summer, saying that he felt like the luckiest man on earth, that when God made me, He had created a safety net for him.

Ashton's incident with that girl had been a major wake-up call. For the past year, I had been trying to right the ship—any issue he'd raised I was actively addressing. I hadn't been drinking for ten months. I was focusing more on my own projects: I was producing a show; I had a wonderful film, *Margin Call*, due out in the fall; and my television directorial debut was scheduled to air the same month. Ashton, meanwhile, was starting a new sitcom, *Two and a Half Men*, which alleviated some of his financial anxiety after the 2008 crash. (He was replacing Charlie Sheen, and would be starring with Jon Cryer. Small world.) I believed we were both working toward protecting what we had.

I was still desperate to have a baby with him. I had finally overcome the huge obstacle of my resistance to using an egg donor. I started scouring the agency lists for the right fit, sharing the most promising prospects with Ashton, and hearing his thoughts. We were in Idaho for the Fourth of July holiday when I found a donor who was a perfect match. I showed Ashton her picture. He said we should go for it.

That was on Tuesday. On Thursday we started filling out the paperwork. On Sunday, we were out walking by the river when Ashton told me, "I don't think I can do this, and I don't know if this is working."

I felt like the wind had been knocked out of me. I asked him why he'd let me research a donor, go through this very painful, prolonged process, and make myself vulnerable in this way if he wasn't up for it. His response was simple: "I never thought you'd go through with it."

THE NEXT DAY I went to New York for work. I was producing an interview series called *The Conversation*, hosted by my friend Amanda de Cadenet. I had personally enlisted Lady Gaga, Alicia Keys, and Donna Karan, among others, and I needed to be there. I was frozen. Waiting for Ashton to reach out and make things right.

I flew back to L.A. a week later; we hadn't been speaking. When I got home, our weekly Kabbalah class was in session in the den. I looked at Ashton as I entered the room, and I felt a chill go through me. His eyes were icy, dead. It was like I was seeing the coldest person I'd ever encountered—nothing like the man I fell in love with years earlier. And it was certainly not like looking into the eyes of someone who loved *me*.

That night, he said, "I think I should move out."

"Whoa, whoa, WHOA!" was all I could say. "We're *married*. That's not how we do things. How did this go from us having issues we need to work on to 'I'm moving out'?" I could feel that he was withholding something. I was grasping. "We need to go and talk to somebody," I insisted.

And we did. But it didn't matter. He didn't really want to work on our relationship. He didn't want us to have sex or be at all physical anymore. He was done. *I* was still very much in our marriage, but I was in it alone now. I was still trying to make sense of somebody who two weeks before had sent me an email saying that he was the luckiest man alive. I craved some kind of understanding of what was happening—if it made sense, then I'd be able to let go, if that was the right thing, but as it stood? It was all just too bewildering. I told him that I didn't think he should move out, that I wanted us to work through this privately, together. We agreed: let's keep this between us; let's not be with anyone else until we sort this out—one way or the other.

It was coming up on our sixth anniversary. Danny Masterson was having a bachelor party the same weekend, and Ashton said he wanted to go down to San Diego for the night to be there for it. He went, and when he returned the next day, he said he'd had a great time. To celebrate our anniversary, he took me to the place we went on our first date: to that piece of land he'd bought that held so many of his fantasies. Our time together was strained, and I just felt in my gut there was something he wasn't telling me. It was driving me crazy.

The next day I had to fly back to New York to do press for a project I was really proud of. It was a miniseries for Lifetime called *Five*, composed of five different short films that told stories about breast cancer set in different times and places, directed by five different women. I was one of them. My story was set in the early sixties, at a time when people didn't even speak the word *breast* in public, so awareness of breast cancer was a major problem. One of the most rewarding parts of the experience had been directing a little girl, and trying to tell the story with a lot of attention to her point of view. The first day of shooting, Ashton had sent me a beautiful bouquet on set: soft blue flowers with a card that read, "I believe in you." I couldn't stop thinking about those flowers on the flight to New York.

I was at the Crosby Hotel, about to get my hair and makeup done for the premiere that evening, when I got a Google alert on my phone. "Ashton Kutcher caught cheating" flashed across my screen. At first I assumed that it was more about the previous year's incident, that one of the tabloids had just found a new way to repackage it. But once I clicked on the link, I realized it was brand new. It was about the weekend of our anniversary that had just passed, the night he was in San Diego at the bachelor party. There were quotes from a young blonde replaying Ashton's pickup lines. I felt sick to my stomach: I knew those words. I knew she wasn't lying. "Aren't you married?" she said she'd asked him. To which he replied that he was separated. Then he spent the night with her, got up, and drove home to celebrate his anniversary with his wife.

"Are you fucking kidding me?" is what came out of my mouth when he picked up the phone. By which I meant, How dumb can you get? Did you *want* to get caught? (The truth is, yes, on a subconscious level he probably did.) And what about *me*? Did you really have to put me in this position, *again*? You couldn't at least have found a way to cheat on me quietly—to *privately* break my heart without dragging me through a public gauntlet of humiliation?

He admitted it right away. Then I had to hang up and go walk the red carpet, praying with every step that this information hadn't gone wide yet, that nobody would thrust a microphone in my face and ask how I felt about my husband of six years fucking a twenty-one-year-old he'd been hanging out with in a hot tub the weekend of our anniversary. I really thought I might throw up.

A week after my forty-ninth birthday, on 11/11/11, Ashton moved out. The statement I released through my publicist was brief but perfectly distilled my feelings: "It is with great sadness and a heavy heart that I have decided to end my six-year marriage to Ashton. As a woman, a mother and a wife, there are certain values and vows that I hold sacred, and it is in this spirit that I have chosen to move forward with my life."

CHAPTER 22

Icouldn't eat. I shrank down to ninety-six pounds: skeletal. I started getting blinding headaches. My body hurt all over, and inside of it, my heart was broken. I felt like giving up.

All I could think was, *How did I get here?*

I went away with Rumer for Christmas. I was not in a good place, and I behaved badly. One of her friends was with us, and I was just being a little too flirty in that sad way a woman can sometimes act when she's looking for validation.

I started to misuse migraine medication—nothing crazy, but I was chipping away at something, trying to dig out of my pain.

I found a way.

At that party in my living room in January 2012, I didn't do anything more than anyone else did—Rumer, some friends of hers, some friends of mine. I inhaled some nitrous. I smoked a little spice, which is like man-made pot. It's not like I went wild and overdosed. I just had a weird reaction, a seizure, which is apparently not that uncommon when people do nitrous or "whip-its," the DIY version of the laughing gas you get at the dentist's office.

But on a deeper level, would I even consider doing drugs with my kid there if I were in my right mind? Of course not. I scared Rumer so badly when she saw me there, semiconscious on the floor; she thought I might die in front of her. She was completely freaked out, and after that night she joined her younger sisters in refusing to speak to me.

That was the worst part, by far. Worse than my friends calling 911 before I could sit up and scream, "No!" Worse than all the tabloid headlines blaring "Demi Moore, rushed to the hospital!" Worse than knowing that Ashton would see that story. Worse than my broken heart. Being a mom was the one thing I felt sure I was truly "successful" at in life, but how successful could I be when not one of my children would speak to me?

How did I get here?

I felt villainized by my family. I was angry that my girls weren't showing me any compassion and that Bruce refused to intercede. And I was embarrassed that I'd put myself in this position. They all wanted me to go to rehab, which just seemed nuts to me: I'm going to show up at rehab and say, "My name is Demi and I don't drink and once I did a whip-it"? I knew that the real problem wasn't drugs or alcohol.

I felt so lost, I would wake up in the morning and think,

I don't know what the fuck to do—how do I get through this day? I was in so much pain, physically as well as emotionally, I could barely function. I rarely left the house, except to let the dogs out. That feeling of not being anchored by all of these people's needs and my role as their nurturer was unbearable. Not a lot was going on in my career, and even if there had been, I was too sick to work. I had no choice but just to be with myself, and I hated it.

Is this life? Because if this is it, I'm done.

I knew I had a choice: I could die alone like my dad, or I could *really* ask, *How did I get here?*, and have the courage to face the answers.

HOW DID I get here?

I got here because I had a grandmother who put up with a womanizing husband who was charming and good-looking and charismatic, and she felt like she had no choice but to tolerate it because she married it. She didn't have the education or the independence to free herself, so she made do and taught her daughters to do the same.

I got here because I had a mother who married the love of her life, but then lived in a state of total love-hate dysfunction with him until he ended his own life. She continued to choose men who were more and more abusive to her until the end of her life, and when she died, she had never experienced peace.

I got here because I am the product of a power play by my mom to get my dad back by her side. They did what they always did when they found themselves in trouble: lied. I came into this world already wrapped in a secret, the child of the wrong man. I can't remember a time when I didn't worry, *Is it okay that I'm here?* And it wasn't, really. I was a complication. I spent decades scurrying to justify myself, thinking if I just worked hard enough, maybe I could earn the right to be wherever I was.

I got here because neither of my parents was old enough or wise enough to take care of my brother and me the way that all children are *entitled* to be cared for. They loved us. But they were not capable of putting our needs first. They did not know how to protect us from danger, and they put us in its way over and over again.

I got here because I couldn't bear to face the question: "How does it feel to be whored by your mother for five hundred dollars?"

I got here because I responded to the dizzying lack of safety and the constant change in my childhood by becoming tough and adaptable. I've spent so much of my life accommodating and adapting to new environments—new schools, new people, new directors, new expectations—that making adjustments based on how *I* am or what *I* need was not conceivable. I never learned that. I think I existed in such a state of distrust that I didn't really know how to *be* in the world—in life—comfortably. And so it was very rare that I was totally here for it.

I got here because I tried so hard to be different from my mom that I took care of everyone but myself. I pushed and pushed myself to be the mom my girls needed, the wife Bruce and then Ashton wanted—but what did *I* need? What did *I* want? It was nobody's job but mine to figure that out and demand it. And it was nobody else's job to convince me that I deserved it.

I got here because when I met the man of my dreams, trying to stay close to him became my addiction. Ashton had seemed like the answer to my prayers. But when we met, I had the experience and the preparation to be really committed. For him it was still the journey—he was still figuring out who he was. The thing I didn't fully take into consideration (and who would want to?) when Ashton and I were falling in love is that what was magical to me and what was magical to him may not have been the same thing. I felt connection, communion. He was stepping off of a private plane for the first time and coming into my home, my family, which I'd long since created, and I had a body of well-known work in the very field he aspired to conquer. I was a forty-year-old who had had a big life with a big ex-husband and three children, and Ashton's adult life was just beginning—both his personal life and his career. I didn't see all that because I was inside of it. I just felt like a fifteen-year-old girl hoping somebody liked me—emotions that, if I'd had a safer and healthier upbringing, I might have been able to feel when I actually *was* fifteen.

I got here because I chose men with the same qualities as my dad and my granddad, and I turned myself inside out trying to please them.

I got here because I never dealt with all the rejection and scorn that came my way throughout my career—I couldn't risk what that might feel like if I really took it in. It would be too terrifying, too much of a reinforcement of a much deeper feeling inside me, that someday, somehow, there would be some kind of big powwow, at which everyone would concur: What the fuck is *she* doing here? She's not allowed to be here. She's not good enough. She's dirty. Get her out. Get her *out.*

I got here because from day one I've been wondering, *Is it okay that I'm here?*

And it was finally time for *me* to tell myself: yes.

I GOT TREATMENT. But for the trauma I'd never faced and the codependence that arose from it. My missteps at the party were the symptoms, not the disease. My physical health was deteriorating: it was the last thing I had, and when it started to go, I had no choice but to stop and learn, for the first time, how to digest. I worked with a doctor, going through my life, one piece at a time, breaking it down, so I could start metabolizing everything that had happened.

My kids had given me an ultimatum: we won't speak to you unless you go to rehab. But I went, and they still didn't show up for me. I told them how important it was for them to attend family week—not just for me, but for all of us. But they refused.

After I completed the program, I reached out repeatedly, offering to meet wherever it would be comfortable—with a therapist, whatever. I was rebuffed or ignored. I couldn't get my mind around what I'd done that was so terrible that they would cut me off without even a conversation. Eventually, though, I had to let go. If not having a relationship with me was what was best for my girls then I would accept that, even though it was the last thing I wanted. I had to trust that working on myself was the most healing thing I could do for them. It would be three years before we were able to find our way back to one another.

It hurt me, and it made me mad, but that time with just myself was incredibly empowering. It gave me the chance to learn what life is as *just me*: Not as a mother or a daughter. Not as a wife or a girlfriend. Not as a sex symbol or an actress. It seems like it should be automatic, living as just yourself. But coming from where I came from, being me wasn't even okay the day I was born.

I sat through not getting a call on Christmas, not getting calls on my fiftieth birthday or Mother's Day. No email. Nothing. Not one thing. When I had nothing left to lose, I could finally exhale, stop gripping. I don't think my instinct for caretaking would have allowed me the space to heal if I'd had my family around me. Maybe I needed to be alone to do it, and, without knowing it, they'd given me that opportunity. I had to focus on taking care of myself: getting help for my autoimmune problems, which turned out to be severe; getting treatment for the trauma I had stuffed deep down into my core, where it had started to rot.

One of our collective fears is being alone. Learning that I'm okay with just me was a great gift I was able to give myself. Spending time on my own may not have been exactly what I wanted, but I was okay. I wasn't afraid. I didn't need to rush to fill the space. There was an aspect of that time of isolation that was *for* my healing—which is how I started experimenting with looking at things in general. What if everything hadn't happened *to* me but had happened *for* me? What I learned is that how we hold our experiences is everything.

I'd learned this before. When my mother was dying, I found a way to change the way I held our relationship. I had spent years facing her with anger and longing: *Why didn't you love me enough to be better?* I'd managed to move to compassion, and that transition had liberated me. Taking responsibility for your own reaction is the gateway to freedom.

I'd learned this with my mother, sure. But that didn't mean applying the lesson again would be easy. Some things just seem too painful to reframe. But if I really look at my difficulty with not being able to get pregnant, for instance, whether I could or I couldn't is irrelevant: it's the judgment I made against myself that was so damaging. If I'm holding it as *I'm a failure as a woman*, of course it's going to destroy me. What if I look at it differently? What if it was for the best, not being tied to Ashton with a child? When I opened my mind to that possibility, I was able to hold it peacefully.

This doesn't mean that now I'm Saint Demi and I have no pain. It just means I can finally admit that I have weaknesses and needs and that it's *okay to ask for help.* I can't fix everything. I can feel sorrow and self-doubt and pain and know that those are just feelings, and like everything else in this life, they will pass.

WASN'T THERE AN easier way to learn all of this? Couldn't I have gotten to this place without Ashton walking out, *and* the kids not speaking to me, *and* my health deteriorating? Obviously not. Any one of those things would have been enough for most people to stop and say, "I need to take a look at myself," but for me it took the extreme of losing my husband, our baby, my fertility, my daughters, my friendship with their father, and not having a career to hide in. Thank God it didn't take losing my home, too.

Things happen in life to get our attention—to make us wake up. What does it say that I had to lose so much before I could break down enough to rebuild? I think it says that the thing that got me here, this incredible toughness, was almost the thing that did me in. I got to a place where I could no longer just muscle through. I could either bend, or break.

I got here because I needed *all of this* to become who I am now. I had been holding on to so many misconceptions about myself, all my life: that I wasn't valuable. That I didn't really deserve to be anywhere good—whether that meant in a loving relationship, on my own terms, or in a great film with actors I respected, who knew what they were doing. The narrative I believed was that I was unworthy and contaminated. And it wasn't true.

There are two reasons I wanted to tell this story, the story of how I learned to surrender. First, because it's *mine*. It doesn't belong to the tabloids or my mom or the men I've married or the people who've loved or hated my movies or even my children. My story is mine alone; I'm the only one who was there for all of it, and I decided to claim the power to tell it on my own terms.

The second reason is that even though it's mine, maybe some part of this story is yours, too. I've had extraordinary luck in this life: both bad and good. Putting it all down in writing makes me realize how crazy a lot of it has been, how improbable. But we all suffer, and we all triumph, and we all get to choose how we hold both.

EPILOGUE

I believe Paulo Coelho was right: the universe conspires to give you everything you want, but not always in the way you expect it.

Christmas is my favorite holiday, and I make a big deal of it. I try to use it as a reminder to play, to be childlike, to make room for a certain magic and joy in thoughtful giving. I know my mom always wanted to make Christmas special for us when Morgan and I were kids. She wasn't capable of pulling it off consistently, but she did manage to maintain one ritual, and I've adopted it: everyone gets to open one present on Christmas Eve—and I always make it funny matching pajamas. (This year it was fuzzy reindeer onesies.) I feel like I'm able to carry out what Ginny started but couldn't finish.

When my daughters weren't speaking to me, for the first time I was able to *feel* what Ginny must have felt when I shut her out of my life. How could I expect them to have compassion for me when for so many years, I hadn't had any for my mother? As I fully heal the relationship with my mom in my heart, it has made way for a depth of loving and closeness with Rumer, Scout, and Tallulah that is even beyond what I thought was possible. We have been able to let go of the misperceptions and judgments that had been trapping us. I've always held the goal that as adults my children wouldn't spend time with me out of obligation—that if they were with me, it was because there was nowhere else they'd rather be. All three of my daughters were here this winter in Idaho.

We were a ragtag crew. I have a furry family of eight dogs and a cat, plus Rumer brought her cat and her two dogs, Scout and Tallulah each brought a dog, and so did my friend Eric Buterbaugh. Eric is my gay husband—it may not be romantic, but it is a marriage filled with love. I have someone who shows up for me and my kids, no matter what, and who shares my passion for clothes and design. There is no one else I would trust with my table settings. I have a mismatched collection of souvenir state plates, and somehow, he always finds a way of elevating them—this Christmas, he interspersed them with his signature "flexed" roses, which he meticulously opens by hand, one petal at a time.

Sarah Jane, Sheri-O, and Hunter were here, along with my friend Masha, another single mom—like Sheri and me—who brought her two-year-old daughter, Rumi, one of the great loves of my life.

Masha is Serbian—from a former communist-occupied country—and not used to the abundance of packages we have under the tree. She found something really profound and lovely to give us: she had an artist draw pictures for each of us, based on Masha's observations. Mine depicts a queen, and the subtext is about me being able to let myself wear the crown.

Hailey is my castle. It's my home, the place where I raised my daughters. It was hard work getting here, but I wouldn't trade what I have with them now for an easier journey. We all took separate paths, but we've ended up in the same place. After what we went through, we no longer take our relationships for granted. Bruce is back in my life now, too, a valued friend and cherished family member. My daughters have two new little sisters—Mabel and Evelyn, Emma and Bruce's kids—and so our family continues to grow. I'm so grateful we all have one another.

I'm grateful to Ashton, too, believe it or not. Whatever pain we went through together enabled both of us to grow into the people we are today. We continue to collaborate with our foundation, Thorn, and I'm so proud of the work we do.

SOMETIMES IN WINTER, it feels like you are inside a snow globe at our house in Hailey. The backside of the house is mostly glass, facing the trees that lead to the river, with the snow-covered mountains rising up behind them. The big flakes fall fast and white, blanketing the natural world, making everything look different—beautiful, peaceful, changed.

Everyone scattered for New Year's Eve, and I stayed there

at the house by myself. There was a full moon in the sky that night, and I felt like a full person looking up at it. I didn't need to jet off to a party. I didn't need a date. I felt I had everything I needed.

I belong. Here, in myself, in this house, on this planet.

I am in my mid-fifties now. I've outlived both of my parents. I know that what I walked through was a lot. Especially coming from where I came from. The truth is, the only way out is in.

ACKNOWLEDGMENTS

Ariel Levy: There are no words to describe my gratitude to you for helping make this book a reality. You saw all the pieces as gems and showed me through your mastery how to weave them into a tapestry. Your excitement gave me permission to find joy; your staggering intelligence and direct no-nonsense simplicity helped me navigate the uncertainties and leave the fear behind. And your understanding and compassion made way for me to let the truth flow. Thank YOU. You are a beautiful human, a kindred spirit, and I thank the universe for bringing our paths together.

Jennifer Barth: This has been a nine-year journey, and through the ups, the crash, and the miracle of completion, you have stood by me, allowing me the dignity of my own process, even graciously offering to let me walk away if needed—placing me and my best interests above the book. I am so grateful it was your office I was swept into that day. You are a magnificent editor, intelligent, extraordinarily skilled, detailed beyond normal human reasoning; but it is your humanity, your understanding as a woman, as a mother, a sister, a daughter, that you poured into the countless, tireless hours together, for which I am most grateful. Thank you.

Luke Janklow: You are the embodiment of ease and grace.

ACKNOWLEDGMENTS

This book truly would not have been written without you. From the beginning you believed in me and my story even when I didn't. You held the space for me to do this when the pain was so great, I couldn't even consider opening the door again. You have gently walked me through this process knowing when to step in and when to step back, but perhaps the greatest gift that you have given me was the comfort of knowing that you were there for me if I needed you. You brought solution and positivity to every twist and turn, keeping everything absolutely manageable: you made hard easy, difficult doable, and impossible laughable. Thank you for going on this ride with me. I hope I have made you proud.

Claire Dippel: We all know Luke would not be Luke without you. Thank you for bringing your joyous smile every day as we moved into your conference room and especially for keeping a steady flow of Red Bull coming my way!

Hunter Reinking: Where to begin? From day one, over twenty-five years ago, you have gone above and beyond; you have been by my side through countless films, two divorces, and the night shift caring for my mother in her final days. My gratitude for you comes from the depths of my soul and is bigger than I could ever put into words. You have brought your humor, heart, and a healthy dose of loving sarcasm along with your powerful work ethic into more late nights and long days than I can count. I love and adore you and truly don't know what I would do without you in my life.

Lenny Hernandez: You are perhaps the sweetest, most kind human I have ever met. There is no task too great or small for you, and no matter what I bring to the table, you meet it with a smile, a joy, an excitement, that spills over with appreciation. You are pure loving kindness and you bring that into everything you do. I am in awe! If I were to learn tomorrow that you are indeed an angel, a saint, a bodhisattva living among us, I would not be surprised. I am blessed to have you in my life. You make so much possible for me, and I could not be more grateful.

Andrea Diaz: I know where Lenny gets it because you are an angel! You are the love glue that keeps my house, my dogs, my life, together. I love, respect, and have the greatest admiration for you. Truth is, I would be lost without you, and so would Little Man, Diego, Minky, Nibby, Harlow, Merple, and Sousci Tunia!

Jason, Merritt, and the boys: Thank you for extending your home, your heart, your family, surrounding me with your love and support. Your guest room will forever be my room, and if you're looking for the key, I still have it!

Glenda Bailey, my fellow Scorpio: You are my teacher, my friend, and one of the most spectacular people I have ever met. Your generosity and kindness are matched only by the depth of your love and integrity. Thank you for seeing me, supporting and believing in me. I am so grateful for you! You make my heart sing with Joy.

My team: Meredith and Carrie, thank you for helping me carry this into the light.

Kevin Huvane: For showing up for me, loving me, and generally being my knight. I love you!

Dr. Habib Sadeghi: You met a little bird with broken wings who was dying and showed her she could fly again—maybe even higher than she ever has. I would not be standing today, let alone having written a book, without you. You have opened my eyes, reignited my soul, and let my heart sing. I am grateful for you beyond words.

John Kenyon: You were my first responder, my lifeline of truth, and my beacon of sanity as I crawled out of the rubble. My deepest heartfelt thanks to you for holding that rope and never letting go.

Sat Hari: When nothing made sense and no answers could be found, you were there, unwavering, with care and loving kindness, nursing me one IV at a time. You are a friend, a teacher, a student, and a fellow adventurer. Thank you for walking this path with me.

Kevin Dowling: Your healing hands and loving heart carried me through!

Tej Khalsa: Showing up to your class and being of service to you gave my life purpose and meaning when I had none. I am so grateful for you and for the breath of life you blew my way.

Ron and Mary Hulnick: I hope through my actions, my words, my deeds, I will show you my gratitude by carrying forward your beautiful teachings in a way that is authentically me. You have touched so many, and I am ever so grateful to now be counted among them. Thank you!

Morgan, my 6'3" little brother: We may not have the comfort of a mother or a father, but I am ever so grateful we have each other. Thank you for giving your love and time to venture into the good, bad, and exceptionally ugly parts of our lives for this book. Love you!

Aunt DeAnna: You have been there for me when no one was. To say I am grateful for you is an understatement. You are a gift, a pure example of loving kindness, and we should all aspire to be as generous and selfless as you are! Thank you for answering every call, hunting down details, filling in blanks, and bringing out old pictures. I love you.

Uncle George: Morgan and I were blessed to have you in our lives not just as an uncle but as a brother who looked out for us like a father when ours was gone. Your insights added so much color and flavor to a part of my mom and dad that no one else could have given me. I am so grateful.

Aunt Billie and Aunt Choc: Thank you for filling in the gaps of love, life, and loss, and for bringing my mom even closer by you being near. I love you.

The Sewing Bee: GP, Jenni, Jen, Sara, Brig, Daun—love you.

Lena D: You are magic.

Peggy, Heather, Guyo, Michelle: You were there. Love you!

Masha and my beloved Rumi Lou: I am overflowing with gratitude to you and to the universe for bringing you both into my life. For allowing me the privilege to be part of your lives, to witness the magic and growth of this incredible little being you have created. Rumi, I will forever be your "Mi," and you can have sleepovers and playtime whenever you want. I love you!

Greta and Linda: You lifted, surrounded, and protected me without even knowing the gift you were bestowing—especially upholding the joy and magic of Christmas! I will forever be grateful.

Eric B: You are a masterpiece, the best gay husband a girl could ever ask for, and a partner for life. So grateful for you. Love you madly!

ACKNOWLEDGMENTS

Sheri-O: They say when the shit hits the fan you know who your friends are. . . . Well, it did, and you were there 100 percent. I am one of your biggest fans and ever so grateful you and SJ are not only friends but family. Thank you for hunting down photos to bring this story more vividly to life.

Laura Day: There are few whose words of advice I value more than yours. You are and have always been my champion. You look out for me with a mother's watchful eye and at times have protected me even from myself. We are friends, we are family, and when needed, we are the mothers neither of us has. I am so honored and blessed to be part of your beautiful, magical Circle. You would move mountains for those you love, and you do. Thank you for believing in me and this book. I love you!

To my magnificent daughters, Ru, Scouter, and Boo: My loves, my angels, my reason for everything, to witness you each growing and unfolding in your own time in your own ways into the glorious, dynamic, majestic, intelligent, loving, caring, compassionate, beautiful women you are today takes my breath away. Thank you for allowing me with your love, support, and encouragement the space to do this book. This is my story, and I know that in sharing my experience, it may not have fully expressed yours or captured the nuances of your pain, fear, or triumphs. That is for you to share. I am so grateful you chose me to be your mother; it is an honor, a blessing, and the greatest gift I have ever received. There are so many stories yet for us to tell, lessons still to be learned, and love still to be shared. And I can't wait to continue our adventure. I Love You!